HAVING

FUN

BEING

YOURSELF

First printing — February 1975
Second printing — June 1975
Third printing — October 1975
Fourth printing — March 1976
Fifth printing — October 1976
Sixth printing — June 1977
Seventh printing — September 1979

Copyright © 1975, by Communication Unlimited. All rights reserved. Printed in the United States of America. No part of this publication may be reproduced, stored in a retrieval system, or transmitted, in any form or by any means, electronic, mechanical, photocopying, recording, or otherwise without the prior written permission of the publisher.

HAVING FUN BEING YOURSELF

TABLE OF CONTENTS

		Page
DEDICATION		4
PREFACE		5
INTRODUCTION		11
I.	Who Am I and Who Are You?	22
II.	Where Are You Going?	36
III.	Am I Four Different Selves?	48
IV.	Do I Have a Healthy Personality?	54
V.	Will People Like Me If I Am Really Myself?	56
VI.	How Can I Know Myself Through Knowing My Values?	68
VII.	Am I a Cupfiller or a Candlelighter?	72
VIII.	Can I Communicate Through Listening?	86
IX.	How Can T.A. Help Me Communicate Better?	108
X.	How Can I Effectively Deal With Conflict?	116
XI.	Does All This "Psychology Stuff" Really Work in Life?	124
XII.	How Does "Being Yourself" Jive With Religion?	142
XIII.	"Try It, You May Like It"	150
APPENDIX		
	Ways to "Have Fun Being Yourself"	163
GETTING IN THE LAST WORD		177
THANKS TO EVERYDAY PEOPLE		181
BOOKS YOU MAY FIND HELPFUL		183

BIRTHDAY DEDICATION

"People who need people are still the luckiest people in the world." I would like to dedicate the "Birthday Edition" of this book to the people I need and not in any particular order of priority because I need them all.

To my long time friend, John, who really organized me and made the first printing a reality. To Mom & Dad, who still create a "no place like home" atmosphere. To Fran, who holds so many things together. To Kevin & Kenny, my two little boys, whom I loved to "freeze" at their young age. To Anni, who held Communication Unlimited together in its infancy. To my boyhood pal, Tony, with whom I spent many fun times, including a night in the detention home. To Buddy, who made my high school days so exciting. To the Efanti and Muro families who made our neighborhood so much fun while growing up. To Red and Dee, my good friends and next door neighbors. To Kay, who creates such a relaxed atmosphere. To Marge, who is an open, honest, and alert friend and helped Communication Unlimited get off the ground in 1973. To Ms Penny who loves little kids. To Fred, a super friend and trainer. To Pat, who gave me so many ideas in the business world. To Shirley, whose challenging personality keeps me on my toes. To Tom, a real thinker and philosopher. To Don, who helped me sidestep a lot of University bureaucracy. To Mac, the best education boss I ever worked for. To Hughes, a super thinker and good friend. To Father Moynihan, the essence of acceptance and "freedom to be oneself." To Bill, who dropped in from Missoula, Montana, and said: "Slow down, Jim, or you won't beat stress and live longer." To Margie, whose life changed because she applied the message in this book. To Luanne, who may someday work with us. To Sam, whom I met the other day and who may join us in our effort to help others become free enough to have fun being themselves. To John, a thinker, an open person, a friend, as well as a brother. To my brother, Joe, who taught me that "B.S.ing" can be fun. To Herb, a real super guy and good friend. To Judy and Linda, my loveable friends from Loveland, to "Tiger" my Hawaiian friend. To Bernie, Paul & Bubbles, three fun people. To those I'd like to put in, but can't think of right now. To the people I have met and will meet in my classes and seminars. I love the give-take relationships. You learn from me and I learn from you, and in doing so we all grow and learn to have fun being ourselves.

A BIRTHDAY PREFACE

HAVING FUN BEING YOURSELF deserves a birthday celebration on the occasion of its seventh printing. The new cover and pictures by Suzanne Novak are the birthday presents. Actually, the birthday being celebrated is the birth of a new book, B.S.* AND LIVE LONGER (* BEAT STRESS). It was conceived in Little Rock, Arkansas, when Dr. Thomas Smith picked up a copy of HAVING FUN BEING YOURSELF. Three weeks later he wrote, "I have been looking for a readable book for my patients and found it in your book. You see, in my experience as a gastroenterologist I can see that the major cause of trouble in my patients is not physical. It is stress and your book is a great stress reducer."

This was the turning point for Communication Unlimited. Two years later, we put out B.S.* AND LIVE LONGER (*BEAT STRESS). Since then we have become deeply involved in stress management and stress reduction work. Our emphasis had previously been on preventative mental health. However, after one fatal coronary, you really have to be a dynamic teacher to help a person's mental health! With one and a half million heart attacks annually in the United States, we feel it is urgent to share stress-coping tools that can enable people to stay alive and live life to the fullest.

This book deals with a major stress generator, because you cannot have fun being yourself if you are "boxed in" by stress. Now that we have become aware of the essential and significant relationship between HAVING FUN BEING YOURSELF and stress, we are adding a few pages in this preface to help you determine if you are a "stress coper" or a "stress carrier". This is extremely relevant because you will be able to have fun being yourself only to the degree that you are able to become a "stress coper".

ARE YOU A STRESS COPER OR A STRESS CARRIER?

"You are the cause of your own stress." If the statement is true, it means that you choose to "carry" stress or to "cope" with stress. We are looking at an either - or - choice. We either cope with stress - or we carry it.

Profile of "Stress Carriers." All of us need clues to see where we fit into the picture. The following are the clues which identify "stress carriers":

1. **Cupfiller.** Cupfillers know all the answers, and have the "right" answers according to them. They utilize their energies by attempting to remake everyone according to their own image and liking.

2. **Good Winners - Poor Losers.** These carriers have the need to be No. 1 in everything. Their world falls apart when they are in a losing situation. Since being "No. 1" in all things is an "impossible dream," the Poor Loser collects a lot of stress in pursuit of this unrealistic goal.

3. **Hurry Sickness.** These "carriers" are always rushing. Waiting in traffic, or in lines, sends them into orbit. They are impatient, irritable, and frustrated. When speaking - or listening - to someone who speaks slowly, "hurriers" tend to finish sentences for them.

4. **Possessors.** Possessors hold on to their power and authority. They just can't delegate. They can't trust anyone to do the job like they do it. This characteristic accounts for a lot of collected stress. It ends up in work overload for possessors, because they just can't do everything themselves.

5. **Producers.** Their feeling of well-being is contingent on doing and producing. In essence, these "carriers" have conditional self-love. They love themselves only when they are **doing** something. Their resulting drive to produce and to "do, do, do" is another reason why they collect and carry stress.

6. **No. 1's.** They have the drive to be No. 1 in everything. Nothing will stand in their way in their insatiable drive to get to the top. When two or more of these "carriers" are gathered together in the same company, the infamous "dog-eat-dog" competition takes place, because each wants to be "top dog."

7. **The Unfulfilled.** Although these "carriers" are not usually aware of it, they are unfulfilled. They are never

really happy and never satisfied. A typical carrier is just as unsatisfied as an executive as he/she was as a beginner.

8. **Guilty-As-Charged.** They cannot take time out for themselves without charging themselves with wasting time in the first degree. Since they lack interior self-worth, they just can't "waste time" on themselves without collecting guilt feelings and stress.

9. **Ulterior Praisers.** These "carriers" praise themselves indirectly by criticizing others. They put themselves up to putting others down. What they are saying is: "No one can do the job like me." This attitude creates poor relationships with others - another source of their stress - because they never gain the sense of belonging, which is a basic need for happiness.

10. **Ceiling-Hitters.** When things don't go their way, they hit the ceiling. They are professional and effective stress collectors. They have a low toleration for anything that is not perfect (according to their perception). They frequently fly off the handle in dealing with others - which creates loads of stress on everyone involved.

11. **Self-Containers.** Asking another for help or advice is beyond the scope of these "carriers." Their value system won't permit it, since they see asking for help from others as a "put down" to themselves. This attitude about getting help from others causes self-contained "carriers" to be lonely and friendless.

12. **"Communique"-ers.** These "carriers" do not communicate. They order, command, threaten, and advise. They see themselves on top, looking down on others. Their parent-child type of communique is the generator of loads of stress in their dealings with others.

These characteristics sum up the profile of the "stress carriers." They certainly provide a rationale for the storage of stress. Now let's look at the "stress copers."

Profile of "Stress Copers." The "coper" is quite different from the "carrier." He works just as hard, but the thrust of his effort is toward "Being" rather than "Doing." The "copers" have a philosophy of life. They know what they want in life and spend time going after it. The following characteristics make up the profile of the "copers":

1. **Candlelighter.** These "copers" have a philosophy of life, but it is open to change. As a result, they feel they can learn from everyone they meet. This attitude creates a sense of worth in the people whose lives they touch. Instead of filling others' cups by trying to remake them, they light others' candles by learning from them.

2. **Unique Winners.** For these "copers" life is not a win-lose battle. Their drive is just to be themselves, and in these efforts there is neither competition nor stress. They are winners in their mistakes because they learn to grow from them. This winning philosophy of "goof and grow" creates a relaxed atmosphere with others.

3. **Hang-Loosers.** These "copers" have learned the skill of coping with a fast-moving society. For instance, George, a "coper," sees time driving, as time alone. If there is a half-hour delay in traffic, it means extra time alone instead of extra stress.

4. **"Share"-ers.** The "copers" accept realistic limits. They realize they can't do everything; so they share their power and authority with others. In so doing they instill a sense of trust in others. At the same time they side-step the overwhelming stress inherent in the "doing-every-thing-myself-if-I-want-it-done" attitude.

5. **"Be"-ers.** "Being" is of a higher priority than "doing" for the "copers." They have learned to value themselves unconditionally. They love themselves for their creative uniqueness and not because of their production out-put. This attitude creates serenity and peacefulness in themselves, which helps them cope so effectively with stress.

6. **Top Person.** Instead of driving to be the "top dog," these "copers" shoot for being a top person. Being your own person eliminates all competition because personhood is essentially unique. By daily becoming aware of their many facets, qualities and gifts, they untap their own potential and find joy and fulfillment in the art of self-actualization.

7. **Contented.** For these "copers," the fulfillment and contentedness flows from their identity goals taking priority over role goals. They search to find out who they are and choose roles which fit their identity. Consequently, they do a lot of the things they really want to do in life. This brings them consistent peace and happiness which is lacking in those who live to fulfill others' expectations.

8. **Rose Smellers.** These "copers" can definitely stop and smell the roses. They can "waste" time on themselves without feeling guilty. They know that being with someone they like is not a waste of time. Rose smellers have learned to really like themselves.

9. **Positive Image Builders.** They look for the good in others and let them know about it. Reinforcing the positive aspects of others makes them feel good about themselves. Helping others to like themselves is one of their rewarding goals.

10. **Realists.** These "copers" have a realistic concept of human nature. They realize no one is perfect, including themselves. This attitude creates a high acceptance level of others which prevents them from hitting the ceiling whenever things don't go as planned.

11. **Other-Oriented.** These "copers" hold that a "person needs others to become one's self." Since self-actualization, or becoming themselves, is so important, they have a sense of belonging and friendships with others. This creates a support system so vital to effectively cope with stress.

12. **Communicators.** Communication is the art of creating a common union with others. This is exactly what these "copers" do. Unimpressed by roles, they look upon others just like themselves, as members of the human race.

Take Your Choice. You now have the profile of both the "stress carriers" and the "stress copers." Actually, every person has to make the choice in terms of what he/she wants to be. In reality, life is not black and white, but gray. We all have characteristics of both "carriers" and "copers." Happiness can be increased, however, in proportion to the ability we have, or can develop, toward becoming "stress copers" rather than "stress carriers."

Read carefully the following poem. When the meaning of this poem becomes a reality in your life, you will know that you are a "stress coper" and you will experience the joy of "Having fun being yourself."

A FREEDOM FIGHTER

Don't make me conform
to your decree
of what you deem
I ought to be.
You expect me to think
As though I were you;
And want me to see
As your eyes do.

What claim do you have
to transmute my design
or pry in a world
That is only mine?
I can't be possessed;
I have to be free!
Why aren't you content
Just to let me be me.

    unknown

INTRODUCTION

Recently a teacher was talking to a group of educators at a conference. Apparently the subject was psychology. He said, "Most psychology books that I have read either dazzle you with brilliance or baffle you with bullshit." The immediate laughter of the group seemed to be saying, "Amen, Brother!" It made me think of the frequent remark of parents who say, "The trouble with your schools is this psychology stuff." It seems safe to say that there is a credibility gap in the field of psychology for a number of people.

I really feel that there are a lot of neat things in the field of psychology that can actually help the everyday person live a more fulfilling life. This book is an attempt to place the principles of humanistic psychology within the reach of the everyday person. Hopefully, it will narrow the credibility gap between psychology and the everyday person.

SUPERMARKET OR BANQUET APPROACH

The best way to approach this book is the way you shop at the supermarket. You look over everything, but take what fits you, what you like, what will help you become more yourself. You are a unique person, you know what you need and what you want. I want to share, but I don't want to walk in your mind.

Actually, I prepared this book just the way I would prepare a gourmet dinner. In the past few years I have run across some "suppers" that I personally really liked. I've collected all these neat things and put them on the banquet table. Look them over, take a little of the things that you may like. Take a lot of the things that you definitely know you like. Remember this is a free flowing banquet, so you are not forced to take anything at all. If you feel forced, you may get sick and not return to the banquet. In fact, you don't even have to clean your plate. If you thought you might have liked something, but didn't, just leave it on the plate. Take and take freely only those things that may help you to help others to grow.

The freedom of the supermarket or banquet approach is essential because you are unique. Also it is a lot of fun picking out those things that will help you to know more about who you are and what you want to do with the precious gift of your life.

WHAT IS "BEING YOURSELF"?

Not too long ago I met a "do your own thing" person. He said, "The only person that I have to worry about in life is me." He said it so dogmatically that it was clear that he had arrived and knew exactly what the "good life" was. I've met a number of these "authoritarian liberals" who seem to grossly misinterpret what it is to be yourself.

To avoid confusion I would like to describe the meaning of "being yourself" as used in this book. Actually, being yourself in terms of a wholesome personality means trying to know yourself as a unique person and insisting on your right to be yourself without trampling over the rights and feelings of anyone else. Moreover, it avoids the two extremes. On the one extreme is the authoritarian liberal who does his own thing regardless of the rights and feelings of others. On the other extreme is the role player who lives his life entirely according to the wishes and expectations of others. Right in the middle between the two extremes is the person who is "having fun being him or herself." The triangle below may make it clearer.

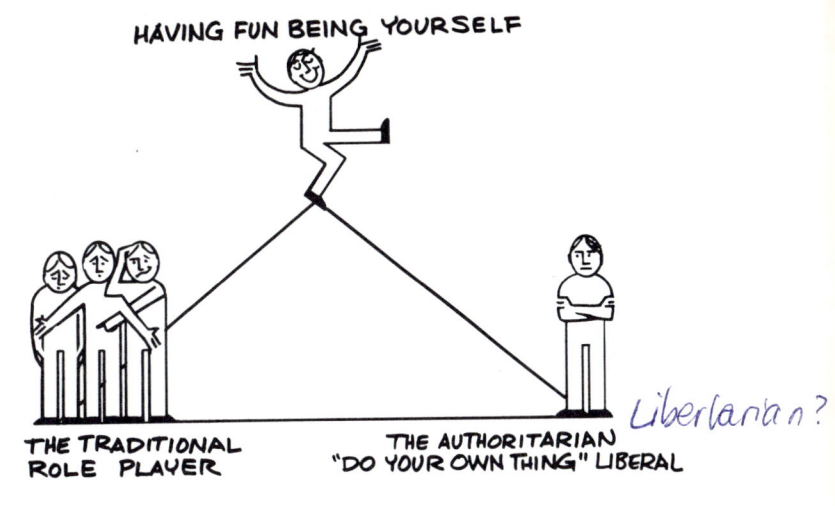

HAVING FUN BEING YOURSELF

Liberlarian?

THE TRADITIONAL ROLE PLAYER

THE AUTHORITARIAN "DO YOUR OWN THING" LIBERAL

There is a famous Latin saying: "In media stat veritas." It means "the truth stands in the middle between two extremes." Notice that truth is at the top above the two erroneous extremes. This book is aimed at the truth. Hopefully, the truth will make you free to have fun being yourself.

HIGH IQ AND LOW FQ

Recently a beautiful college girl with an A average jumped off a cliff to her death. In America thirty teenagers commit suicide each day. Why? They have poor F.Q.'s. This book is based on the assumption that there are many people who have sufficient I.Q.'s to meet the challenges of daily living, but have low F.Q.'s which seems to be more necessary to cope with today's world. In contrast to I.Q. (Intelligence Quotient), F.Q. means Feeling Quotient. "F.Q." was coined by my good friend John Roughan. It refers to the ability to be aware of one's feelings coupled with

13

the capability to handle them. The college girl who committed suicide most probably did not have feelings of worth as a person (F.Q.) even though she had a good mind (I.Q.). A good F.Q. means that you feel good about yourself as a lovable and capable person.

In a workshop the other day, a woman volunteered for the demonstration on active listening. We were listening to her feelings on love. She said that recently she had met someone who really likes himself as a person. She said, "He is so secure in himself, that he lets me be myself." She went on to say that, "This person can love others because he loves himself. He has it all put together. If someone doesn't love himself, he can't love others." What she is saying is that the person has a high "F.Q." The moral of the story is, raise your F.Q. by knowing yourself, loving yourself, and you'll really begin loving others and having fun being yourself.

REASONS FOR WRITING

Before I read a book I like to know something about it. I page through the foreword and read the table of contents to find out whether I would find it worthwhile for me to read. I may save you a lot of trouble if I share the reasons for writing this book.

IT'S BEING ME

I am the kind of fellow who wants to share things with others. Fortunately, over the years I've encountered some really neat things that have helped me live a fuller and richer life. Since I see myself as a sharing person, I am just "being me" by taking out time to get these things all together and share them with you.

IT'S PRACTICAL

I teach a number of enhancing self-concept courses. I have one course for teachers, one for married couples and another for re-entry into the single life. I also do government workshops on communication around the country. Never could I find a book to fit my style and fit my course. At last I have this book that attempts to say what I really think is important in helping people feel good about themselves and live life to the fullest.

Also, being somewhat disorganized and mislaying class notes, I really feel secure having thousands of copies of my notes within the safe covers of this book.

WRITTEN FOR THE EVERYDAY PERSON

I am writing this book for the everyday person. Everyday "slang-spiced" English is my style. I avoid big words, footnotes, etc. Since I grew up among city firemen (my Dad, two brothers and two nephews are all firemen), I use "fireman" language which is definitely understandable to the ordinary person.

PREVENTATIVE APPROACH

The axiom "an ounce of prevention is worth a pound of cure" is a fundamental assumption in this book. I attempt to use solid psychological approaches for the ordinary normal individual. In my courses at the University I assist the good teacher to become better; help a good marriage become a better marriage. In this book the identical approach is used: i.e., you are good, you're effective, but you can become better; you can live a more fulfilled and satisfying life.

IT'S "PSYCHOLOGY ON THE HOOF"

I coined this expression to point out that some principles of psychology can help people live fuller lives. I have taken many psychology classes and often came out filled to the brim with high level theory. I was so frustrated with "theory overload" that I had to sift through it and keep only that which I could apply to my own life and that of the everyday person.

THE SUBJECT IS **YOU**

You are the subject of this book. How to be a better "you" is what it's all about. Anyone can be alive, but to "live" is a talent that comes from knowing yourself.

A former student named Max describes this book better than I do. For years Max wrote poetry, but never dared share it with anyone. It was so much a part of him, so close to him that he feared others would reject his poetry and thereby reject him. In a book written for ordinary people, it seems fitting to include a poem by an ordinary fellow.

MYSELF

Myself is a baffling thing tis true
But without it I wouldn't be missing much,
While others think I'd be missing much,
I am quite contented you see.

For while some find me strange and truly unique
And often repulsive it's true.
But if people could order myself I'm afraid
I might end up exactly like you.

Now don't get me wrong, you're a wonderful guy,
And I find you quite charming it's true.
But can you visualize what the world would be like
If there were two of you?

So God in His infinite wisdom and might
Devised a remarkable plan.
By giving each one a self of his own,
He made us an individual man.

COURAGE FIRST, HAVING FUN LATER

"Having fun being yourself" is really the second step. The first step is "getting courage to be yourself." Somehow a person must arrive at a "yes" answer to the question: "Will others accept me if I start being me?" This is a risky question to ask and more risky to answer. Once you come through that barrier and realize that you are a Good Person and you really like "you," then you can have fun being you. It is fun because the more you become "you," the more you learn about "you." It is fun in terms of a "rewarding" feeling, an "at-one-ness" feeling you acquire when you are "you" — nothing more, nothing less, just you. All the money in the world could not buy that "rewarding" feeling.

Another poem by another ordinary person may help you drum up the courage to be you.

COURAGE OF COMMUNICATION

A "moment" lost may well an eternity be
as to be but a breath past.

*That word unspoken, or thought held silent,
   leaves its instant unembraced.*

*T'were better for me if that moment had
   never come;
for pained am I its beauty unsavoured,
   its love
unknown, its ray of hope extinguished
   and forever gone.*

*In the twinkling of an eye lies the
   fullness of time
never to be recaptured.*

This poem makes me think of some of the peak experiences of my life which were nearly "almosts." I often think of what I would have missed if I had left "that word unspoken" or "the thought held silent." I don't even want to think of what I missed when I felt in the old days that "the word unspoken" was the virtuous thing to do. I've tried to adopt the ideas of this poem. They have given me renewed courage not to lose that ever present "moment." Perhaps these ideas will do the same for you.

NOW IS THE HOUR

Now is the hour not to say goodbye but to say "Hello," to "Come Alive." Within the covers of this book are ideas that have really enriched my "Now." I also know that they have enriched the lives of people in my classes who tried to use them in their lives. Hopefully, this book may enrich your "Now" by making you somewhat aware of who you are and where you may want to go.

I would feel well rewarded if most of the people who read this book became aware of the reality that "There never was or ever will be anyone just like you," and perhaps your greatest contribution to this world is to find out who you are and share your uniqueness with the world. This would enrich your life and also make the world a little better than you found it.

ACT NOW, TOMORROW MAY NEVER COME

You may find a lot of things in this book that you would like to try in your life. I suggest that you try them now. No one is assured of a tomorrow. In a recent lecture at the University of Northern Colorado, Dr. Leo Buscaglia brought this point home by quoting an anonymous poem by one of his former students. It went something like this:

When we went to a dance, I forgot to tell him it was formal. He showed up in jeans. I thought he would get mad, but he didn't.

When I dropped strawberry pie on the new carpet of his car, I thought he would kill me, but he didn't.

When I flirted with other guys, I thought he would drop me, but he didn't.

When I dented the fender of his new car, I thought that he would bawl me out, but he didn't.

When I forgot about a date we had, I thought he would get sore, but he didn't.

When we had to spend a whole day with my little sister, I thought he would get furious, but he didn't.

When I lost his engagement ring, I thought he would disown me, but he didn't.

When he came home from Viet Nam, I was going to tell him how much I appreciated and loved him,

BUT HE DIDN'T.

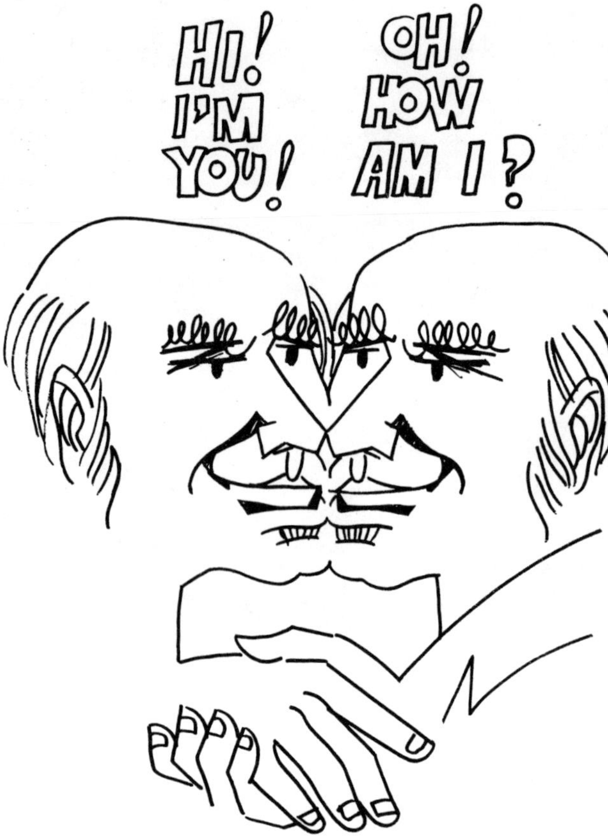
HI! I'M YOU!
OH! HOW AM I?

CHAPTER 1

WHO AM I AND WHO ARE YOU?

In September, 1970, I started the doctoral program at the University of Northern Colorado, thanks to a graduate assistantship. I enrolled in a class in Humanistic Psychology and "lo and behold" the teacher took the first hour or so of class to share his background. He happened to become the best psychology teacher I have ever had--and maybe sharing his humanness was a big part of it. He never put himself above anyone. He, too, was just a member of the human race. For me this was a "peak experience" in learning in the field of education. Looking back I see that 26 years of my life (more than half my life) was spent in school. Dick Usher was the first teacher who took time out to share himself as a person with the class. Later I found it was more than just chance. He had done research to find out that the most effective tool of the teacher is not his writings, his intelligence, his degrees, but himself. It actually is the person of the teacher and the atmosphere he sets that produces an ideal or less than ideal learning environment. At any rate, I was so impressed with Dick's personalistic approach, that I have adopted it. Before every class, every workshop, I take time to share a little bit about "who am I?" Hopefully, you'll get more from this book if you know a little bit about me.

1. Who Am I?

In January of l930, I appeared on the scene. My Dad is as Irish as a four leaf clover and my Mother is a warm people-person German. I grew up in North Denver — known as a rough-tough part of town. Like a lot of kids

I played the role of a tough guy and an Athlete (known as "jocks" by today's generation). The series of events in my life point out the fact that my life was definitely determined by my values. I valued the role of being tough, and I was.

A RIDE IN THE LAUNDRY TRUCK

Actually we didn't get into too much trouble with the law. However, one night we, my brother Joe and I plus our Italian friends, Tony and Pat, were playing cards when Billy, an eighth grade drop-out, honked the horn outside. "How about going for a ride?" he shouted. We jumped in to find (several blocks later) that he had stolen the Capitol Laundry truck that we were riding in. We all played the "I'm not chicken" role and spent the next several hours taking turns driving. However, on our way home about 11:00 p.m. two police cars pulled us over. Tony and I quietly tried to sneak out the back door until the policeman grabbed us with the words, "Where are you going?" We replied, "It's such a nice evening, Officer, that we thought we'd take a walk." Incidentally, Tony is now a juvenile officer. This was his inservice training.

At the police station we were waiting for questioning which we called the third degree. One policeman gave us some chewing gum and we thought that he was really neat. They took my brother Joe first. They asked him where he was at a certain date, and implied that he might have stolen some things from a filling station. They picked the wrong man. Joe could out talk anyone. Very indignantly he gave the questioners a lecture after they called him a liar. "Do you realize that I am not only a Catholic at St. Pat's school, but an altar boy — and altar boys don't lie — dammit." Joe wore them out so that we didn't get questioned at all.

THE BEST ALTAR BOYS

They took us to the "Holiday Inn" as I like to call it. Others called it the detention home. It was a little scary, but it certainly was a learning experience. The next day was December 8, 1943, the feast of the Immaculate Conception, a big day in the Catholic Church. However, Fr. Barry, the Irish priest at St. Pat's had no altar boys for the 7:00 a.m. mass. They were all in jail. In no time, Fr. Barry was down at the detention home. He told them: "You can't keep these boys here — they are my best altar boys." I often wondered what they thought his worst ones were. He said, "Jimmie, me lad, did ya steal the truck?" "No, Father," I replied. "Okay, give the keys back and let's go," said he. On December 8th, we were sprung. For two weeks my classmates wouldn't talk to me because their parents told them to stay away from Jimmy cause he steals cars. Later I broke the role barrier of a car thief.

FOOTBALL AND NO. 1

Just like today, we wanted to be number one in football. As a result, we traveled across town to St. Joe's, known for its championship football teams. The blood, sweat, and tears that went into football practice was living proof that being a championship football team was a major value in our lives. Since then I have changed values, but at that time my value for football enabled me to take a lot of knocks physically.

PARTIES OR STUDIES

Study really wasn't a big value in our gang. First of all, if I had brought a book home I might have endangered my role of a tough guy and could have been classified as an "egg head"- a title which I didn't care for. Secondly, I really was content to just coast by in school with a minimum of effort spiced with a little copying when the answers were really tough.

The time we didn't use in studies released us for more interesting endeavors like parties, jitterbugging, hotrods, and drinking beer. Our motivation grew with each party. My high school chum named Buddy was a real fun-loving guy. Neither of us was a candidate for the National Honor Society, but both of us really enjoyed high school (although we were considered the most likely not to succeed). We kept our minds active in school by planning and executing intricate practical jokes. We never got caught, but one joke had a reverse effect.

THE JOKE THAT BACKFIRED

It was graduation year- 1947. Buddy said, "Let's play a joke on the gang." I replied, "Impossible, they know us to well." He said that it would work because he figured it all out. Everyone was talking about their plans after graduation. All we had to do was to think of something different and tell them that we were going into that field. We thought and thought. The craziest idea that we could come up with was to tell them that we wanted to be like Fr. Schwartz, our athletic director, an ex-football player who became a priest. Leaving a career in football to become a priest was like going from a GS 17 in the government to a GS 20. From our teenager value system, we looked at anyone who went to the "Priest Factory" as someone who couldn't find anyone to marry and just couldn't hack it in the world. It really seemed like an "out of sight" idea. After a party, Buddy sprang the news on the gang. They rolled in the aisles. One gal named Pat said, "My God, if you and Jimmie become priests, I'm going to become a nun." Well, of all the gang, she was in no way headed in that direction.

THE SEMINARIANS

For some it was so funny, that they called us the seminarians. On our way out of school for a three day suspension, someone remarked, "Aren't the seminarians supposed to give good examples?" The gang didn't fall for the joke, but it did work. Fr. Barry, the priest who sprang us from the detention home, was transferred, and in came Fr. Haas who was really interested in athletics. At one of the games he overheard someone say, "Jimmy, our seminarian, made a touchdown." The next day he was at my door just as enthused as a kid with his first bike. "I hear that you are going to the seminary," he said. I really didn't know how to respond. First of all, it was usually the police department and not the priest at my door. I asked him where he'd heard that. I knew that he'd fallen for the joke, but I wasn't about to tell him that Buddy and I thought that being a priest would be the most idiotic thing we could think of. I finally decided to play along and gradually he would forget about it. However, he came out regularly and took me for coffee and doughnuts, games, picnics, etc. I told Buddy. He laughed and asked, "Why don't you tell the poor guy?" I told him, "You're crazy, Buddy, I'll keep up the free treats he gives me. I'll tell him in June when I get another job somewhere. This is real North Denver Diplomacy." In June I told him that I had a nice job and changed my mind. He accepted it graciously. That was the end of the "Free-bees," but my diplomacy worked.

THE NEW AMSTERDAM CASUALTY COMPANY

I was offered a job at the New Amsterdam Insurance Company because they wanted a male typist. Buddy and I decided to join the typing class because there were forty girls in the class and they looked lonely. Buddy had a short attention span—he couldn't keep his eyes on the keys—and got kicked out. I kept my eyes on the keys and girls at the same time and made it. So there I was at the insurance company. At best I could type 16 words a minute with 15 mistakes. I later became the greatest casualty that they ever had by misfiling many of their policies. They hadn't asked me if I knew the alphabet before giving me some filing duties.

THE NEGATIVE COUNSELOR

I had never met a counselor. I had learned to type and so ended up in an insurance company. Certainly not a planned vocation. However, I feel that we can learn from good experiences as well as from bummers. My negative counselor, an insurance agent, was a real bummer. He thought that there were four persons in God, and he was the fourth person. He played such a superior role that I felt like sliding him down the linen chute. However, he occasioned my first four real thoughts in life (I went through school with a perfect record—no thoughts).

THE JOKE BACKFIRED

After an encounter with this agent, I had my first four significant thoughts. It was the last of August and football was in the air. My first thought was depressing — no more football — I graduated. My second thought was, "I guess that I'm going to be in insurance." My third one was, "If I stay here, eventually I'll become an insurance agent like the phony agent that irritates me." I said to my self, "In no way." So I quit. Then I thought of Fr. Haas whom I got to know by accident. I said, "He isn't a phony. He's neat. He's always around sports. He likes kids. I like sports. I like kids. Therefore, I am going to be a priest."

SHE LOCKED THE KITCHEN DOOR

That very day I went home to tell my mother. She locked the kitchen door and said, "Sshh ... I won't tell anyone. If this is another joke, tell me." I really couldn't blame my Mom because of my infamous background of joking. I told her that I was going to give it a try because of that phony insurance agent. I mentioned that if I liked it, I'd stay. If not, I'd quit. The next day I told my girlfriend. Needless to say, that didn't set too well because I'm sure that she planned to be in the ring race of '47. At that time a girl was an old maid if she were single at 19. However, she was married in several months. She was good looking and well built — my value system at that time. Thank God that we didn't get married, because we were so temperamentally different that it just wouldn't have lasted.

A VERB FROM A VEGETABLE

I took the entrance exam for the seminary. I flunked the English part. I was angry and surprised. I told them, "English is my best subject — I talk it all the time." However, I had to go to Regis College a year to make up the English. I really didn't know a verb from a vegetable. After a year I learned enough to get into the seminary.

I studied for three months. Then I smuggled a squirt gun into the room. I shot my roommates. Soon they had one in self defense. Then we went to other rooms during study periods. Sometimes it ended by throwing buckets of water. I got more interested in jokes than studying and my grades went down proportionately. I quit at the end of the year before they could kick me out. I was back with the old gang and Buddy. Both of our girlfriends were in nurses' training. I forgot about the seminary when a new parish priest, Fr. McQuire, came out and talked me into trying out in the Marists, a religious educational order. He got me interested by telling me that they were good athletes. I gave them a chance. I spent one year in Pennsylvania, one year in New York, two years in Boston, and four years in Washington, D.C. In 1957 I made it.

POPE IN FOUR YEARS

I returned to Denver and neighbors said, "Jimmy, are you really a priest? What's happened to the Catholic Church?" I told them that I would be Pope in four years. Never reached my goal. I was assigned to San Rafael, California, where I coached football, basketball, and baseball. Among other things, I also taught English. It wasn't too long after that before they asked how would I like to go to a parish? Where? Hawaii. I said, "I'll take it."

I loved Hawaii. I was assistant pastor in charge of youth. I loved it. In fact, my values began to change. I would have liked to have had some youth (children) of my own. Just about that time, Good Pope John came on the scene. He believed in shared decision making, he started to break the paternalistic approach of the church. He wanted things to be on an adult-to-adult level instead of a parent-child level. It looked as if everyone was going to have something to say in the Church. The whole atmosphere was changing. I belonged to a group of young priests who were working for change in the Church, and it looked as if married clergy were right around the corner. Then John died and Paul came in. Immediately it was clear. Paul seemed to have a different type of shared decision making than John. Paul made the decisions and shared the results. Hopes of a married clergy and shared decision making started to fade.

TAKING A STAND: A TURNING POINT

After a year of thinking it over, I resigned in 1968. I went to Colorado University for another degree in counseling and psychology. However, actually I was looking for someone to marry. My values had changed. I had done a lot of marriage counseling, and saw that it was easy to say "I do" but traumatic to say later "I don't." My main criteria was someone who liked children and someone who was flexible. I saw myself as free wheeling and not too organized, so I needed a flexible person for compatibility. I ended up with a 'ringer'! I was just about ready to zero in on my number one choice when Fran came on to the scene. She is flexible and she likes kids. We now have two "altar boys," Kevin and Kenny. I'm raising altar boys instead of training them.

THE UNION CARD

After working as a high school counselor (which involved more paperwork than counseling), I was at the right place at the right time and got a grant to study for a doctorate or the "Union Card." To teach on the university level a person needs the "Union Card." The doctorate doesn't make you a good teacher, but you can't qualify without it.

TEACHING TEACHERS COMMUNICATION

After the doctorate program, I got a job teaching teachers how to communicate with children. This means how to enhance the self-concept of the children through communication. What a challenging job. People often ask why teachers need such a course since they are trained in the university to work with children. Actually, they are given a few courses in psychology. However, too many times the saying of a friend of mine is truer than its opposite: "Many of my psychology teachers were psychopaths who didn't have the decency to go crazy." Actually, that funny and exaggerated statement may come from the strong opinion that a number of people go into psychology to solve their own problems. Many go into psychology to learn tools to help others. Consequently, the caliber of psychology teachers will vary with their motivation for being in the field of psychology.

COMMUNICATION UNLIMITED

After a year and a half of working for a school district, the increased demand for workshops in education and in the government made me seek a half time contract in the school district. One person "in the know" said there would be no problem. Consequently, I got booked up for a lot of workshops. Finally I put in my request. Surprisingly it was refused on the ground that it would set a precedent. No one had ever gone from a full to a half time contract in the history of the school district. I asked to talk to the school decision-making cabinet. They said that they wouldn't change. Fran and I decided that we had enough to make the house payments until May—then the sun shines—who needs a house? In February, 1974, I resigned and began "Communication Unlimited." At present it is one year old and, thank God, I'm going strong. The hardest part is to keep the workshop dates straight since neither Fran nor I is good at organization and planning.

RETIRED

I see myself as retired because I had planned to do communication workshops when I retired. The refusal of the half-time contract forced me into early retirement (15 years before my original retirement plan). My hobby is communication and it is a really neat feeling to make a living at doing what I like best. I am still working part time as an off-campus instructor for the University of Northern Colorado teaching communication courses, e.g., "Enhancing Self Concept in the Classroom," and "Psychology of Communication in Marriage."

It has been a long interesting ride from the stolen Capital Laundry truck to traveling in airplanes for Communication Unlimited. I have traveled the restricted roads of living up to other's expectations. Now I'm beginning to taste the wonderful experience of living up to my own expectations and it is fun. I'm writing this book because I would like to share this experience with others. Having fun being yourself is an experience in love — and love has to be shared if it is to grow. To keep love, you have to give it away.

2. Who Are You?

One of the best ways to find out is to sit down with a pencil and paper right now and try to answer the question: "Who am I?" This exercise has been done with literally hundreds of people. The following is the most typical response:

1. I am a man.
2. I am a government worker.
3. I am a supervisor.
4. I am a son.
5. I am a husband.
6. I am a father.
7. I am a golfer.
8. I am a sportsfan.
9. I am a brother-in-law.
10. I am an American.

This person, and by far almost all of the people who answered this question, answered in terms of roles. Two more questions are necessary to see the impact of this.

WHAT DO ROLES TELL OTHERS ABOUT YOU?

You are a man, but the world is crowded with men. You are a government worker, but there are thousands of government workers. You are a supervisor—there are thousands of supervisors. You are a son, but every male born is also a son. You are a husband, but every married man is a husband. You are a father, but every man that had children is a father. You are a golfer, but there are loads of golfers. You are a sportsfan, but there are millions of sportsfans. You are a brother-in-law, but there are oodles of brothers-in-law. You are an American, but the U.S. is full of Americans.

The answer is obvious. These roles don't tell others anything at all about you. This leads to the next question.

WHAT DO ROLES TELL YOU ABOUT YOURSELF?

Take a minute or two to think about this question. The answer seems clear. It tells you as much about yourself as it tells others about you. NOTHING! The difference between your role and yourself is tremendous.

THE CONCLUSION IS FRIGHTENING

If most people respond to the question "who am I" by using roles, then it means that most people know very little about themselves. Most of my life I personally defined myself by roles, e.g., I was a football player, a North Denverite, a Catholic, an altar boy, a party-boy, a seminarian, a college student, a priest, a youth director. My last goal was to be pastor, another role. For me roles meant living up to other people's expectations. I was so busy playing roles that I didn't know who I was or where I wanted to go.

I have the feeling that many people are still caught up in playing roles. They are where I was. In the covers of this book are ways that have helped me and others switch from roles to identity; from where other people want you to go, to where you would like to go. Hopefully there are things on the supermarket shelves of this book that can help you gain some insight into who you are and where you want to go.

RICHMAN
POORMAN
ASTRONAUT
ACTOR
HARVARD
PLUMBER
PILOT
YALE
POLITICIAN
FIREMAN
BEGGARMAN
THIEF
RAH!
DOCTOR
LAWYER
MERCHANT
TEACHER
CHIEF
MILITARY
SERVICE
BUS DRIVER

CHAPTER II

WHERE ARE YOU GOING?

A recent study indicated that more than half of the college graduates eventually end up in a field different from that for which they were trained. Why? Perhaps the best answer is that most college students never took the time to find out who they are before they decided where they wanted to go. Educators recently have become aware of the vital connection between knowing who you are and effectively deciding where you want to go. A recent vocational education project funded by the federal government has its main thrust in helping the students to find out who they are as the basis for deciding where they want to go.

WHO ARE YOU?

Somewhere along the line some alert educator said that we are products of our environment or culture. Because we live in a role oriented culture, most of us are probably running around with large roles and small identities as pictured below.

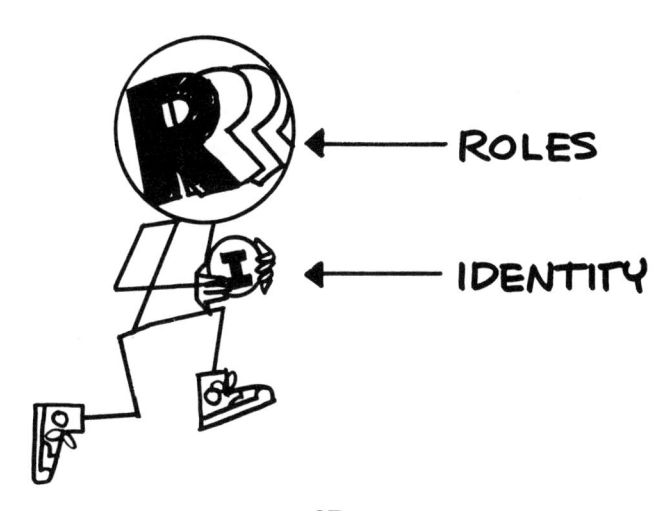

← ROLES

← IDENTITY

BIG ROLE—SMALL IDENTITY

The unhappy person represents those who are top heavy on roles due to our role oriented society. How many times have you heard or even said, "Make something of yourself," "Go to college and be someone." This, of course, refers to a higher and better role. On the other hand, how many times have you heard, "Be yourself." Rarely, if ever.

SOCIETY REWARDS ROLES

Unfortunately, we are rewarded for playing roles from the time we are born, e.g., be a good boy, be a good student, be a good father, be a good mother, be a good P.T.A president. No one ever seems to reward us for just being ourselves. In fact, sometimes we are scolded for being ourselves because it is not in line with our role expectations.

ROLES ARE NECESSARY BUT DANGEROUS

Roles are necessary for the smooth functioning of society. Fathers, mothers, policemen, firemen, engineers are all roles with defined privileges and responsibilities. Roles are essential to make a society. They become dangerous to the formation of a healthy personality when they become top heavy and smother one's identity. When people see themselves as a role instead of a unique person, they are in trouble. Recent studies have shown that many men die within three years after their retirement. In my opinion, the principle reason is the fact that they invested their entire worth in their role. When they were no longer a policeman, or a fireman, they lost their worth because they lost their role. The trauma in retirement seems to be due to the fact that people's identity rests entirely on their role. They retire from their role and they lose their sense of identity, their sense of dignity and worth. They become nobodies because their "Being someone" was dependent on their role instead of their uniqueness and identity as a person.

ROLES COME FROM "OUGHTS"

If you stop to think about the origin of roles, you will clearly see that they are nothing else but organized "oughts." To be a good boy, you ought to do this. A good mother ought to do this. A good father ought to do this. The trick in life is not to be smothered by the oughts, to keep plenty of breathing space in your role to be yourself. If for some reason there is not room in your role to be you, you might well think about switching to a role where there is room to be yourself.

If you become smothered by roles, this means that there isn't any room either to find yourself or to be yourself. Since roles come essentially from others' expectations, the role player spends his/her life living up to others' expectations. The "Time pie" (see Appendix) has been helpful in increasing awareness of one's role playing. Two months ago a young girl, 22 years old, did the "time pie." She was amazed at the small slice left for herself as a person. In a matter of several weeks she really changed. She now has half the pie for herself as a person. Everyone in the class noticed how she blossomed. The ways to be yourself (see Appendix) are certainly helpful in the process of shifting gears from roles to being yourself.

ROLES ARE DECEIVING LITTLE DEVILS

Roles actually can't bring happiness, but they certainly can give the appearance of being able to bring happiness. One man pin-pointed how roles fooled him when he said, I thought once I graduated that I'd have it made. I graduated and thought that once I got married, that I'd have it made. I got married and thought that once we had children, I'd be happy. We had children, and I thought that once the kids were grown and on their own, I'd have it made. The kids are gone and I really don't know my wife. Now I'm saying, once the divorce is final, I'll have it made. I'm wondering now if I'll ever have it made or reach happiness."

Role playing can never bring happiness or fulfillment. It over-fills one psychological need and starves the other. We role play because we want to belong, to be accepted by the group. This is a vital psychological need. However, we have a vital psychological need to be unique, to be ourselves. A 'thoroughbred" role player sacrifices the need to be himself in order to belong. He represses his desires, feelings, wishes, because they might be an obstacle to his need to belong. The role player is also a lonely person deep down. He knows that he is playing a role he really never feels liked for himself because no one knows him. People don't like him, they like only the role he plays. This creates a shallow and insecure sense of belonging.

ROLE PLAYING INCREASES PSYCHOLOGICAL CHOLESTEROL

Role playing means repressing our feelings. Repression of feelings creates anxiety or "psychological cholesterol." Psychological cholesterol has probably taken more lives than physical cholesterol. In his book, *The Transparent Self,* Sidney Journard spends one chapter on the lethal role of the male. He seems to attribute the fact that men die earlier than women to the roles that society puts on men, e.g., be a big boy, don't cry, etc. To be a man often means not to express fear or other feelings. This causes psychological cholesterol which in turn causes high blood pressure, ulcers, heart attacks and premature death. Role playing is not healthy psychologically or physically.

ROLES DIVIDE INSTEAD OF UNITE

Identity of person-to-person relationships unite. Role relationships often divide. Not long ago a principal was recalling the time he was promoted from a high school teacher to a coordinator in the school administration building. He was honored to be chosen for the position. He didn't realize that some people were going to change their attitude toward him because of his new role. He could not believe the difference. When he would come to visit his old high school, many of his old friends were aloof and cold. His very association with the administration of the central office now made him a "one of those distrustful guys" instead of a friend and fellow colleague which he recently was before he got his new role.

Another teacher was made principal in the elementary school where he taught. The first time that he walked into the teachers' lounge as principal, he noticed a significant change in attitude of the teachers. They were less joking, more aloof—there was a sense of fear. He said that he could understand why the job of being a principal is a lonely job. Later he was able to break the role and be himself and allow the teachers to be themselves. This is a challenging task for anyone in authority, but it seems to be the best way to create a humanistic atmosphere in schools or in offices.

SWITCHING FROM ROLES TO "BEING ME" TAKES AWARENESS

Step one in the big switch from roles to identity is any awareness that you are playing roles. Last night after class I had a milk shake at McDonald's with three students. One of them shared how the class had made her aware of her role playing. She said, "I have been playing roles all my life and recently I just have become aware of them. I remember as a teenager, I had an intense need to belong, to be part of the gang. If I was walking down the street with two others I would have to get in the middle so that I would be sure that I belonged, that I was in on the action. I have been doing the same thing in my married life with my husband and friends. Last Sunday I made my first big step toward being me. My husband and I went skiing. The people that we went with wanted to have a drink after skiing. Larry and I wanted to go home. I said that I felt tired and was dying to go home, so I'd take a rain check. For the first time in a long time, I said what I felt and did what I felt. It took a lot, but I made it." First she became aware, then she took the first, little (big in her eyes) step toward saying what she felt and doing what she felt.

SWITCHING FROM ROLES TO "BEING ME" TAKES GUTS

Below is the picture of the ideal person in terms of handling the playing a role or "being me" conflict. She doesn't do away with roles or quit society, she just puts her identity or "being me" first and then she lives up to her various roles with the uniqueness of herself.

The woman in the picture has really arrived. She has placed her identity in number one spot and her roles are secondary. She livens up her roles with originality because she brings her "being me" to them. She has

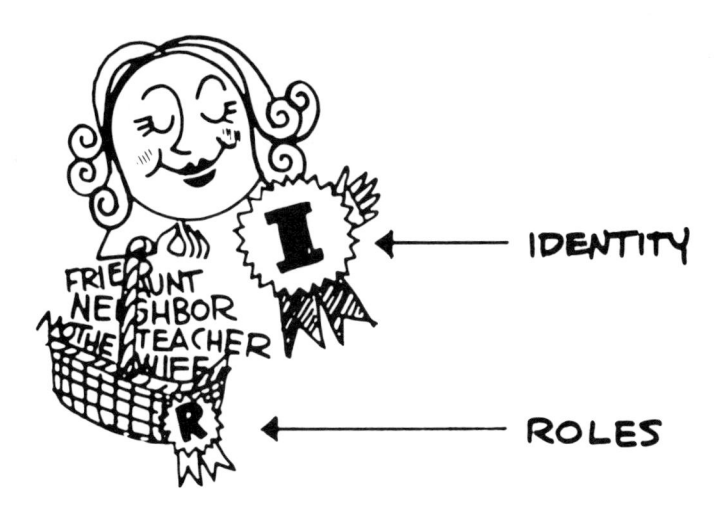

IDENTITY

ROLES

a big smile because she is happy. It is a deep happiness because it is based on the very nature of the person. As some great philosopher said, "Having is in no way a substitute for being." Roles come under the "having" department, e.g., having a GS 10 rating, having a swimming pool, having a country club membership. "Being" strikes at the very core of the person—his uniqueness, his very being, himself.

Last summer a 30 year old teacher in my class heard that I was thinking about creating a class in the "Psychology of Communication in Marriage." I told her that I wanted to be sure that there were enough people to take it before I spent time preparing it. I doubted if she could find that many in her small city. Apparently she really was determined that she and her husband would profit by it, because she rounded up twenty couples to take the class within two weeks. The class took place last summer. The main thrust was creating a person-to-person relationship through the skills of communication.

It took a lot of courage for this woman to put into practice being herself, but it worked. She recently wrote:

This switching from roles to me has really been neat. A month ago I decided to learn to play the piano. Bill thought that the whole idea was a waste of time and money. My feelings were different. I don't give a damn about the money! I want this because I need it for me. I don't care if no one else ever touches it. This is my project. We now have a piano. I'm taking lessons and love it! It is a great way to relax for me. Even my husband now agrees that it was a good move.

My husband is accepting me for what I am. We are both accepting the children for what they are. We are all able to see each other's virtues and much more, accepting one another's shortcomings. We are no longer a threat to ourselves or each other.

All in all, we like being ourselves and having others like us too!

    Much thanks,

    Betty

Betty's marriage got better when she learned to be herself. Unfortunately things don't always turn out that way. This is clear from Carol's letter.

Dear Jim,

The class, "Enhancing Self-Concept in the Classroom," really made me think more about who I am. I was being torn apart. I was accepted as a person at school, but not at home. My husband and I grew further apart. I became more aware of myself, of my interests. I began to like me. It was all right for me to be me. I didn't have to change, to play a role for my husband or anyone else. After much thinking and attempted communication, my husband and I agreed to a trial separation. At this writing it has been four months and the prospects of reconciliation don't look good.

I see myself as a person in my own right instead of a role player. I don't have to be beaten down. My husband doesn't see things as I see them. He just doesn't appreciate the little things that I value. He won't accept me just as "being me." I don't have to change. I want to be me.

How sad for the person that isn't fortunate to find his true being. Even though it has complicated my life, I am grateful. I am enjoying myself, and I am on my way to peace.

Sincerely,

Carol

BEING YOURSELF BALANCES YOUR DIET

Actually, the "thoroughbred" role player is a half-starved person psychologically. He is only half fed. To be full, he has to satisfy his need to belong and also his need to be unique. He only satisfies his need to belong in fulfilling his roles. The picture below may illustrate this.

Probably one the greatest challenges in life is to be able to find enough room to be yourself within the structure of necessary roles in life. We all want to be loved. We want to be accepted. We often repress our real feelings to gain this acceptance. We could gain a lot by thinking about the words of the thinker who said, "In life some people will like us, some may not. We might just as well be ourselves so that we will know who really likes us and who doesn't."

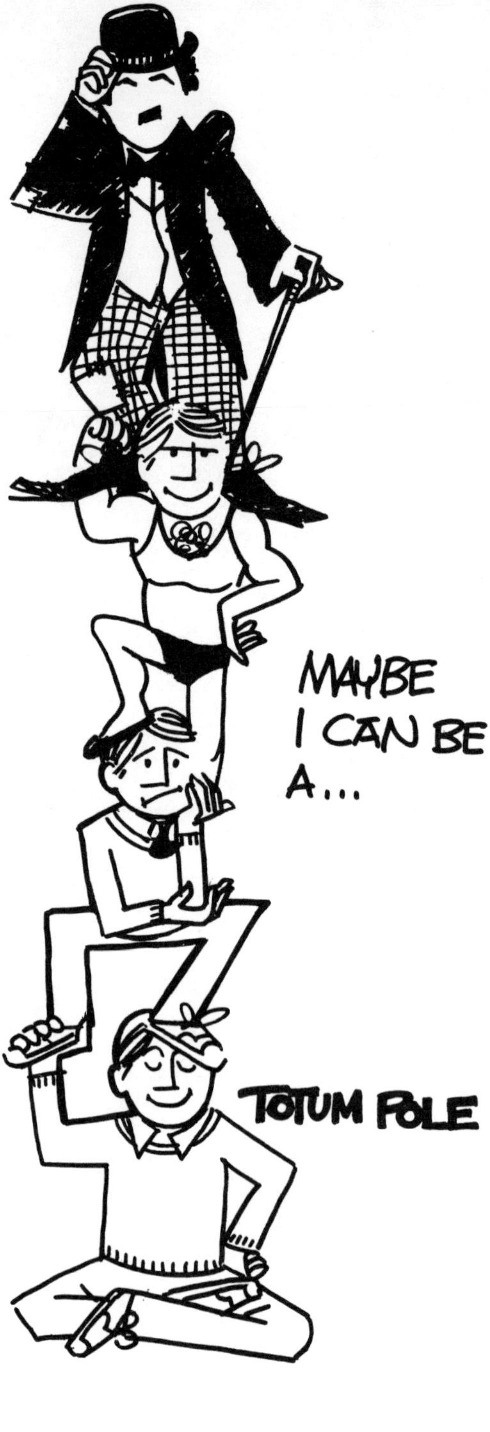
MAYBE
I CAN BE
A...
TOTUM POLE

CHAPTER III

AM I FOUR DIFFERENT SELVES?

Knowing oneself is a life time job. Working on four different selves seems to make it so complex that it would be an "impossible dream." This would seem to be the case but it really isn't. A knowledge of our four selves can be a useful tool in the challenge of learning about who we are and where we want to go.

1. How I See Myself

My self-concept is one self. This self is made up of how I really see myself. This self-view is absolutely essential in my relations towards others. If I see myself as not having anything worth offering, I will not contribute anything to conversations. If I see myself as not being likeable, I'll stay to myself at a party or make excuses to go home early. If I see myself as not being able to remember names I'll not be able to remember people's names. If I see myself as not very smart, I'll never think of going on to college.

On the other hand, if I see myself as having something to offer, I'll try to take part in conversations. If I see myself as likeable, I'll develop friendships. If I see myself as capable of remembering names, I'll remember them. If I see myself as lovable, I'll meet with love.

From this it should be clear that having a wholesome self-concept is essential for having the courage to be yourself. A person with a good self-concept is like a gambler at Las Vegas with $50,000 in chips. He can take the risk of betting $1,000.00 at a crack because he has got a lot backing him. He can take the risk because he has a lot to fall back on even if he blows this one roll. So, too, the person with a solid self-concept . . . he can take the risk of life because he has a lot backing him, his self-confidence. But the poor self concept person is more like the gambler who has only $5.00 worth of chips. He really lacks money to back him up. Likewise, the person with a good self concept can take the risk because he has a lot of self-confidence. On the other hand, the person with the poor self-concept is like the gambler at Las Vegas who has five one dollar chips. He worries and sweats it out before he decides to bet one chip because he has so few.

2. How Others See Me
How others view me is my other self-concept. This has a direct effect on my self-concept. My self concept is formed, to a very great extent, from significant other people in my life, e.g., parents, teachers. For instance, if my parents loved me, listened to me, and gave me a feeling of worth, I probably will have a good self-concept. On the contrary, if they "put me down," told me I'd never amount to much, and told me I was a no good spoiled brat, I most probably will have a low or poor self-concept. Clearly, how others see me has a lot to say about how I see myself.

3. How I Think Others See Me
Too often how others see me and how I think others see me are two different self-concepts. Moreover, it is not how others see me, but how I THINK others see me that really affects my life. In the summer of 1973 there was a "real neat" teacher in the self-concept class. After one activity she said that she was always

afraid to join a group because she saw herself as being rejected. She never made the first move at any gathering because she thought others would reject her. Others, on the contrary, saw her as warm, fun, approachable, friendly, alive and alert. Nevertheless, she acted in accord with how SHE THOUGHT others saw her. In my experience most people's concept of how they think others see them is unfortunately almost always below the concept of how others really see them.

4. How I Would Like To Be

This is another self-concept that is a goal. It usually is like the stars. We can aim at them without quite reaching them. Often there is a big difference between how we see ourselves and how we would like to be. This is clear from the case of a group of junior high teachers. At one workshop activity where there were seven cars to choose from, they went to the car which best represented them. A large group chose the V.W. because they saw themselves as "slow, small, unpretentious, and very common." When asked to go to the car which represented the self they would like to be—almost all of those in the V.W. rushed to the sportscar. The reasons they gave for the change was they would like to be "colorful, flashy, sexy, free, daring, and fun-loving." Basically, they saw themselves caught in the role of a teacher and wanting to break out to be their real selves.

WHAT IS A HEALTHY SELF?

The trick is to take a look at your four selves and get them all together. This is one way of interpreting what the young college kid means when he says "I've got to get it all together." The key could very well be in the following four step plan.

1. Seeing Yourself and Liking What You See— Knowing yourself and acquiring an okay feeling is the first essential step. Some of the ways of doing this are listed in the section in back of this book entitled "Ways to have fun being yourself." No doubt there are other ways. These ways have proven successful for a number of people. After a recent government two day workshop which used some of these ways to have fun being yourself, one participant wrote: "Right now I feel good. I've learned to like myself better. I feel better qualified, and now if someone should ask me 'Who are you?' I will be able to answer more intelligently and honestly." "Feeling good about yourself" is a definite sign that you like yourself.

2. The second step is closing the gap between how others see you and how you think others see you. This is easier to do in a class setting by using some of the ways listed in the back of this book. However, most of them could be adapted to use with your family or your friends. Increased awareness of how others respond to you is a vital source of learning and liking yourself. Perhaps, one of the greatest means of finding out is having one or more friends with whom you can be free to be you and from whom you can get some open and honest reactions to yourself. Thinking that others like us a little when they like us a lot is a mistake that stunts our growth. Thinking that others tolerate us when they actually like us is a personal tragedy which stops growth and often gives us a "not okay" feeling about ourselves.

3. The third step is closing the gap between how we see ourselves and how others see us. Someone once said something like "what a wonderful gift it is to see ourselves as others see us." This sums it up well. If we

have these two self-concepts in line, we are really in a good position to relate effectively to people. In this way we can fulfill two basic needs: the need to love, and the need to be loved. Actually knowing that you see yourself as an "all right" person and knowing that others see you the same way is absolutely crucial for reaching the level of "having fun being yourself."

4. The last step is closing the gap between who you are and who you would like to be. This comes when being yourself really becomes a value in your life. Once being you is essential, you begin to question your life style in terms of freedom to be you. Gradually, you make changes which free you to be you. The changes could be simple like assuring yourself some free time just to do what you want to do. The changes could be major like two teachers who quit teaching after seventeen years to run a lawnmower shop or a housewife who went into teaching because she needed challenge and stimulation from others besides her three little children. The very fact that you become aware of the difference between who you are and who you want to be is a giant step. Just keep the awareness in your mind and you'll find ways to close the gap. When the gap is closing, you'll know it because you'll begin to "have fun being yourself."

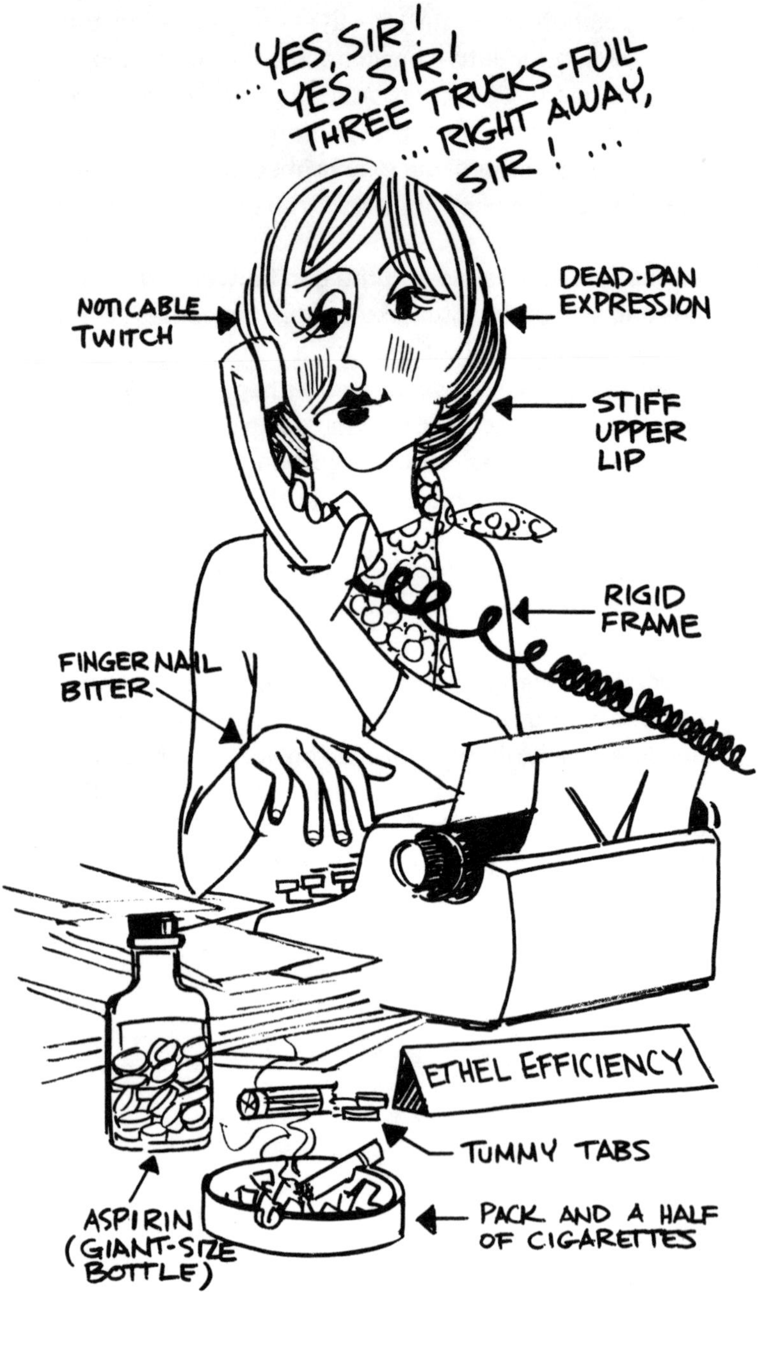

... YES, SIR! YES, SIR! THREE TRUCKS-FULL ... RIGHT AWAY, SIR! ...
DEAD-PAN EXPRESSION
NOTICABLE TWITCH
STIFF UPPER LIP
RIGID FRAME
FINGER NAIL BITER
ETHEL EFFICIENCY
TUMMY TABS
PACK AND A HALF OF CIGARETTES
ASPIRIN (GIANT-SIZE BOTTLE)

CHAPTER IV

DO I HAVE A HEALTHY PERSONALITY?

We all like to know where we stand. We want to know how we are doing everywhere . . . at school, at work, in the family. We get some idea of where we stand in terms of a healthy personality by comparing ourselves with the simple formula or the question approach.

A SIMPLE FORMULA

$$HP = \frac{O}{R} + \frac{AO}{S} + I.S.$$

- HP   means healthy personality
- O   means open
- R   means reality
- AO   means always open
- S   means someone
- IS   means increasing the someones

Taking the formula step by step it means a Healthy Personality is open, but this openness is modified by reality. Being open and honest is definitely a healthy quality. However, it has to be modified to fit reality; e.g., Joe works for an absolutely unreasonable boss. Inside he feels like telling him what he feels like. However, he has 3 children to support and telling his boss off could very well mean losing his job. Consequently, Joe decides to temporarily keep his feelings inside. When he gets home he may share his feelings with his wife or a good friend. In that way, he avoids repressing them. Repression is not good for mental health.

How well I remember the doctoral student who used a different plan. First of all, he had a run-in with his advisor (who is like "his boss"). I'll never forget his telling me, "Jim, I went to a sensitivity course and I learned to say exactly what I feel." (There was a lot of poor sensitivity training at the time.)

A week later he called his advisor a jackass. He could have done it more diplomatically by pointing out the useful role a jackass played in the "Flight into Egypt." The following summer I stopped in to see him while at the University. He was feverishly studying for his comprehensive examinations which he had to re-take because he had flunked them the first time. His openness was not in touch with reality . . . for calling his advisor a jackass and flunking the exams could very well have been a cause and effect situation.

The moral of the story is that openness must be tempered by reality. Straightforward, open and blunt criticism has given a lot of people a not-okay feeling about themselves; the open person was unaware of the situation of the people being bowled over by his bluntness.

The last part of the formula means being open to developing more really good friends. This is based on the assumption that "A person needs others to become himself."

If you have a friend with whom you can freely say what you feel, you have the healthy experience of getting out all your feelings. It has been my experience that when I can do this, I can more clearly "put it all together." In other words, a friend who is a good listener helps you to learn more about yourself as well as more about each other.

Recently, I awoke to the fact that I have good friends in Boston, another in Connecticut and another on an island in the South Pacific. Correspondence doesn't replace the person-to-person talks. Since this awareness dawned on me, I have been working at "increasing the someones" and it has been rewarding.

WHAT IF YOU HAVE NO SOMEONE AT THE MOMENT?

This seems to be the case often in our mobile society. Also, so many people have been "let down" by a friend in the past and are much slower and cautious in developing new friendships. I think it is good to get your feelings out one way or another. You may laugh, but I know several people who just talk to their dog. I know another who sits down and writes down what is on her mind. Others just sit down and talk to themselves. It is wholesome to get your feelings out in some way. The ideal way is a good friend. In the meantime, you can try whatever works best for you.

THE QUESTION APPROACH

The following questions may help you check out yourself in terms of the essential elements of a healthy personality.

1. Am I a happy person?
This means that most of the time you should be essentially happy. If most of the time you are not, you may not be meeting some essential psychological needs.

2. Do I know myself?
This means I have to have a deeper knowledge of myself than simply answering to a title: husband, wife, mother, secretary, etc. Roles don't tell me anything about myself.

3. Do I know where I am going?
Assuming you know who you are, you should be in a good position to decide where you are going. A sense of direction or goals are essential to the healthy person.

4. Do I like myself?
Liking yourself is fundamental. If you see yourself as having worth and something to offer others, you can create many beautiful and growing relationships. However, if you don't like yourself, you may assume that others won't like you either and you may withdraw rather than creating a sense of belonging with others.

5. Do I move away from facades?
This means I don't try to keep up with the Joneses. I'm content to be me, and I don't have to act cool or intelligent or name drop.

6. Do I move away from "oughts"?
This means I feel really free to make a lot of decisions in my life. It means I am not caught in a child-parent relationship where I have to check out what I should do.

7. Do I move away meeting others' expectations?
I may have a long line of teachers in the family and I may be expected to be a teacher also. I may see myself as much more happy being a carpenter because I

love working with my hands. Being a carpenter would be moving away from meeting others' expectations. Being a teacher means conforming to them. I'll never forget the boy who was flunking in medical school because he was there only to please his parents. Once they realized what it was costing him they asked him to transfer, and he became a successful engineer.

8. Do I have a few close friends?
Friends with whom you can be free to be you, to say what you feel seems to be essential for knowing yourself and "having fun being yourself."

9. Am I open to change?
If I am not open to change, then I act like I have arrived. If I act this way, I stop growing as a person. Knowing and being yourself is something you never fully reach. To grow you have to be always willing to change.

10. Can I accept others with different values?
Basically, can I be me and free others to be themselves even though I don't share their values? Essentially it means I accept their right to be different.

11. Do I feel I can learn something from everyone?
Once a person realizes that he can learn something from everyone, the whole world becomes full of learning and growing experiences.

12. Am I as open as circumstances permit?
This means that I try to be as transparent as possible. Openness and honesty is basic in creating wholesome relationships with others.

13. Do I prefer value sharing or deep level conversation?
This means I try, especially with friends, to avoid superficial cocktail level chit-chat in favor of sharing meaningful things as goals, values, and meaningful experiences.

14. Do I have an unhostile sense of humor?
This means I use humor to add joy to life and relax the atmosphere not as a means to get out my hostility by "putting others down." Hostile humor makes lasting impressions. I know a person who is 81 years old and he still remembers the time his eighth grade teacher said: "Joe, where did you get an answer like that? You have a head and so has a pin!"

15. Am I comfortable being alone?
The ability to be alone with just yourself seems to be an important facet of a healthy person. He loves people but loves himself enough to be alone with just himself.

16. Do I have peak experiences?
Since the healthy personality is living life to the fullest, he should have a number of beautiful experiences throughout his life. A long talk with a special friend where you learned something new about yourself can be a peak experience. My little boys, Kenny and Kevin, provide me with many beautiful experiences. They fall asleep in my arms and look just like little angels.

17. Do I share decisions at home and at work?
Sharing decisions goes a long way toward building up the worth and dignity of those with whom you share them. The healthy personality is not

powerpossessive. He shares rather than collects power. In sharing he builds a common union with people.

18. Do I have an accurate perception of reality?
This simply means do I see things as they really are; e.g., telling my boss where to go may mean looking for another job. This means accurate viewing of the real world.

19. Am I spontaneous?
This means can I just be me, or do I have to weigh my every action with "What would they think if I did this now . . . maybe I had better wait." It also includes freshness of appreciation. Perhaps it can be seen by looking at the opposite. One of a group suggested going to the mountains. Another remarked: "Oh, no, I've been there."

20. Do I share my feelings with others?
The healthy person does not use words to hide his feelings. His feelings are a big part of him and he has the ability to share them in his communication with others.

HOW DID I RANK?

Don't worry if you don't feel that you have to have a 100% of all the above qualities. All they are are guidelines letting you in on areas that you may want to get better in. You may be good at all of them, but you also can get better at all of them. You may have a *healthy* personality, but you certainly can have a *healthier* one.

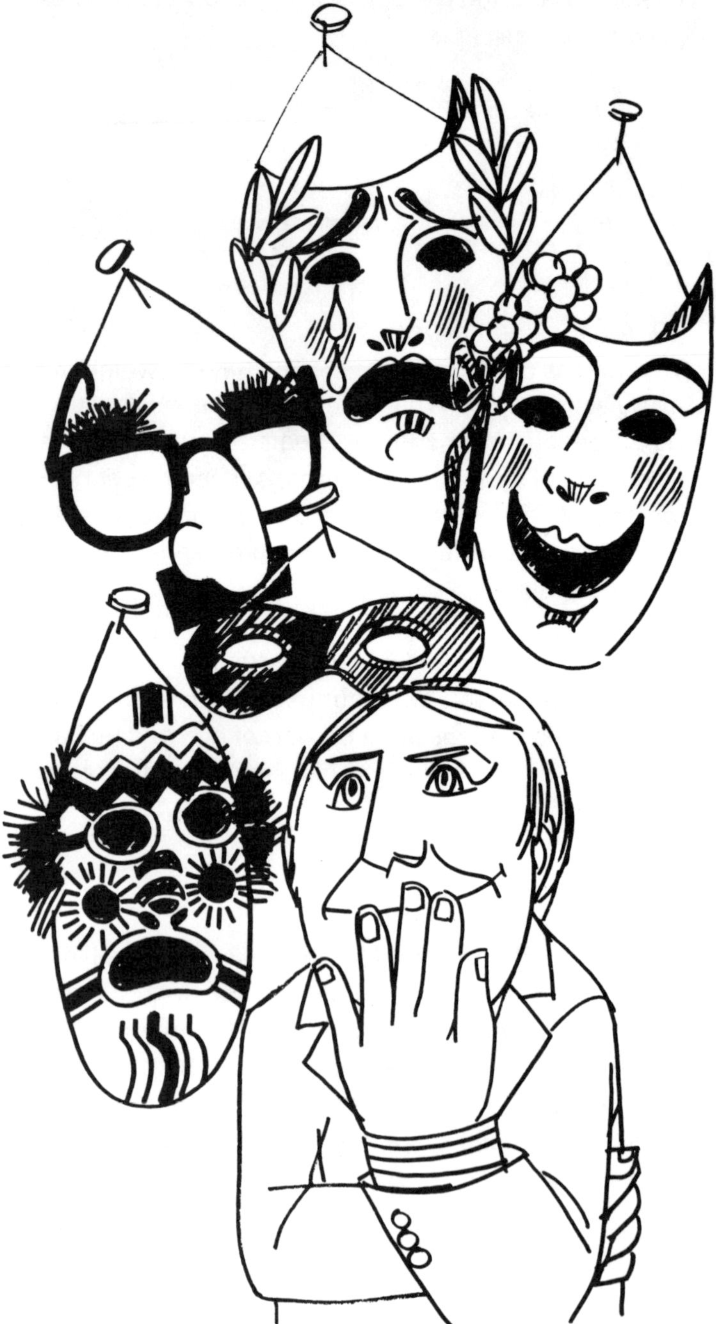

CHAPTER V

WILL OTHERS LIKE ME IF I AM REALLY MYSELF

During a summer workshop in 1974 I found out that one of the students lived near me. So we took turns driving to school and had some interesting talks during the rides. I'll never forget her saying: "Jim, for thirteen years of my marriage I asked myself the question: Will others like me if I am really myself? For all those years the answer was 'No'! So I played the role my husband expected, the role my family expected, and I tried to live up to what his family expected. Finally it got to be too wearing. So I just started to be myself and started to do things the way I like to do them. What a surprise! I found out they liked me as me and I didn't have to play a role. What I like best about the whole thing is the fact that when they react positively to me it means much more now. Before they were reacting to the role I was playing and compliments really didn't mean much."

MOST PEOPLE LIKE YOU TO BE YOURSELF

There are a growing number of people who are finding room in their roles to be themselves. A neat person and new friend in particular is a splendid example. He has an extremely important government position in the civil service training center. He has a lot of the child in his personality. He just loves to do fun things. He works these "fun things" right into his workshops. What he does is certainly not in his role expectations. He, however, really has fun being himself. He also livens up his role as a trainer by bringing his uniqueness to that role. He is extremely well liked because most people like people who have fun being themselves.

IT CAN BE A HIGH RISK

I know a man who after 9 years of marriage decided to stop playing his "good husband" role and began sharing his honest feelings with his wife. To this day she keeps telling him how well she likes the "new you."

However, I know of other cases where one spouse would not accept the person stepping out of the role expectations. When this person tried, she was met with: "You sure have changed, you are not the person I married." The person today is confronted with a non-accepting spouse and is trying to decide whether it is more important to stay in a role-to-role relationship or give up the relationship in favor of just being herself.

IT'S THE ABC'S OF PSYCHOLOGY

I feel it boils down to basic psychology. To be a fulfilled person everyone has to have his basic psychological needs met. If they are not, then they are starving psychologically . . . which is just as real and crippling as starving physically.

People play roles because they want to meet this basic need to belong. They belong when they live up to another's expectations, which is really what role playing is all about. From early childhood through the teens this sense of belonging seems to be overpowering. A little child needs love from his parents and he will live up to their expectations so he can be loved or so he can belong. A typical junior high school teenager will almost "sell his soul" to belong to the gang. Long hair, short hair or no hair, he'll conform to fulfill this basic need to belong. However, this need in early life is usually expensive because the person is giving up another basic need . . . the need to be unique, to be himself. The result is an imbalance of needs or an unbalanced, unfulfilled person as shown in the figure below.

FEELINGS ABOUT SELF

NEED TO BELONG   NEED TO BE UNIQUE

THE FULFILLED PERSON

I speak of the happy or the fulfilled person in terms of someone who has fulfilled in a balanced way his basic needs. This is exemplified by the triangle below.

GOOD FEELINGS ABOUT SELF

NEED TO BELONG   NEED TO BE UNIQUE

This triangle represents the fulfilled person. In being fully himself, he not only did not give up his sense of belonging, but attained authentic belonging because people like him for himself and not for a role. This, of course, automatically fulfills the need everyone has to feel good about oneself. What better feeling could there be than to make one feel "on top of the world" derived from being free to be oneself and still be liked, still having a sense of belonging with others.

A GLAD AND SAD EXPERIENCE

Several months ago I had a "glad-sad" experience. It was at my government workshop on "Group Process and Effective Management." Somehow this one government worker, a woman around forty-five, was sharing a "turning point in her life."

For 45 years I have always kept my real self inside. I was the only one who really knew the real me. I didn't dare bring it out because others would reject my real self. Lately I have started to bring out my real self. I am so happy because others are responding positively to the real me."

I was so glad to hear that she found out that she could be herself and people would like her. I always was saddened to realize that such a beautiful person had to hide her most beautiful part—her unique self.

I am writing this book with the hope that people will start much earlier in life to find out that "It's okay to be me!" and also create an atmosphere allowing and encouraging others to feel 'it's okay to be themselves."

CAREER ★
RELIGION ★★
LOVE ★★★★
HOME ★★
JOB ★
MARRIAGE ★★★★
CAR ★
CHILDREN ★★
RECREATION ★★★

CHAPTER VI

HOW CAN I KNOW MYSELF THROUGH KNOWING MY VALUES?

Just last week my life-long friend was visiting me. He sat in on my "Partners" (see Appendix) during which each partner discusses different topics for minutes at a time. The topic of one such discussion was "What do I like best about myself?" His partner said she felt her greatest likable asset was definitely her ability to listen. She then proceeded to use up the entire time talking about her listening ability without ever listening to what he had to say. She said she valued listening. Her actions indicate that she valued talking much more than listening. There are many examples of lack of real self-knowledge through lack of value awareness. There is the unforgettable principal whose strongest value and motto was that a "child is a candle to be lit and not a cup to be filled." However, his teachers classified him as one of the world's greatest "cupfillers." A typical comment about him: "He talks 59 minutes of every faculty meeting and leaves one minute for input from the rest of the staff." Being unaware of personal values is literally a disaster in terms of growth. The lady mentioned above will never become a listener if she mistakenly thinks that she has already "arrived." The principal, a classic cupfiller, will never become a "candlelighter" because he thinks he's "there" already.

Your basic value system has a tremendous influence on who you are and where you are going. If you have a foggy idea of your values, you'll have a foggy idea of who you are. You'll be aiming at going in one direction and be headed in the opposite.

It's safe to say no one knows all their values perfectly. However, it is also safe to assume that the clearer we know our values the clearer we will know ourselves and where we want to go. In the section at the end of the book you will find "Ways of having fun being yourself." Doing these exercises with yourself or with others should help you get a clearer picture of what your values are and what is important to you.

Doing these exercises has changed the direction of people's lives. Take the example of the government executive secretary. She was divorced for four years and was planning to marry a nice young man. While attending the government workshop on communication, she did the WIN, PLACE, OR SHOW EXERCISE. From this exercise she realized her little boy, Chris (5years old), was an extremely important value in her life. She also began to see a value conflict. The man she was about to marry saw himself as a child raising expert. However, she saw his approach more effective with animal training than children. She cringed every time he would "put Chris in his place" with his harsh orders or his biting "put down" ridicule. She no longer was sure she was going to marry this man. She valued Chris too much to expose him to his "self-concept demotion" approach. She realized that she would have to resolve this value conflict before she could think of marrying this man. She discussed it with him and he wasn't about to change his position. This was the way he was brought up; this type of discipline was good enough for him and would have to be good enough for Christopher. The young secretary made a hard decision but a "value right" one. She liked the security of having a husband, a home, and a family. However, she knew she would spend a lot of her life in utter frustration trying to protect her small son from the "put down" discipline. She knew that this environment would make Chris a very unhappy boy. If he were unhappy, she could not be happy. She made a hard but satisfying decision because she had a chance to see more clearly her values through a simple little exercise WIN, PLACE, OR SHOW.

This real example points out the reality that knowing your values is essential to knowing who you are. Knowing who you are is essential to knowing where you want to go. Knowing where you want to go in life is a great step in HAVING FUN BEING YOURSELF.

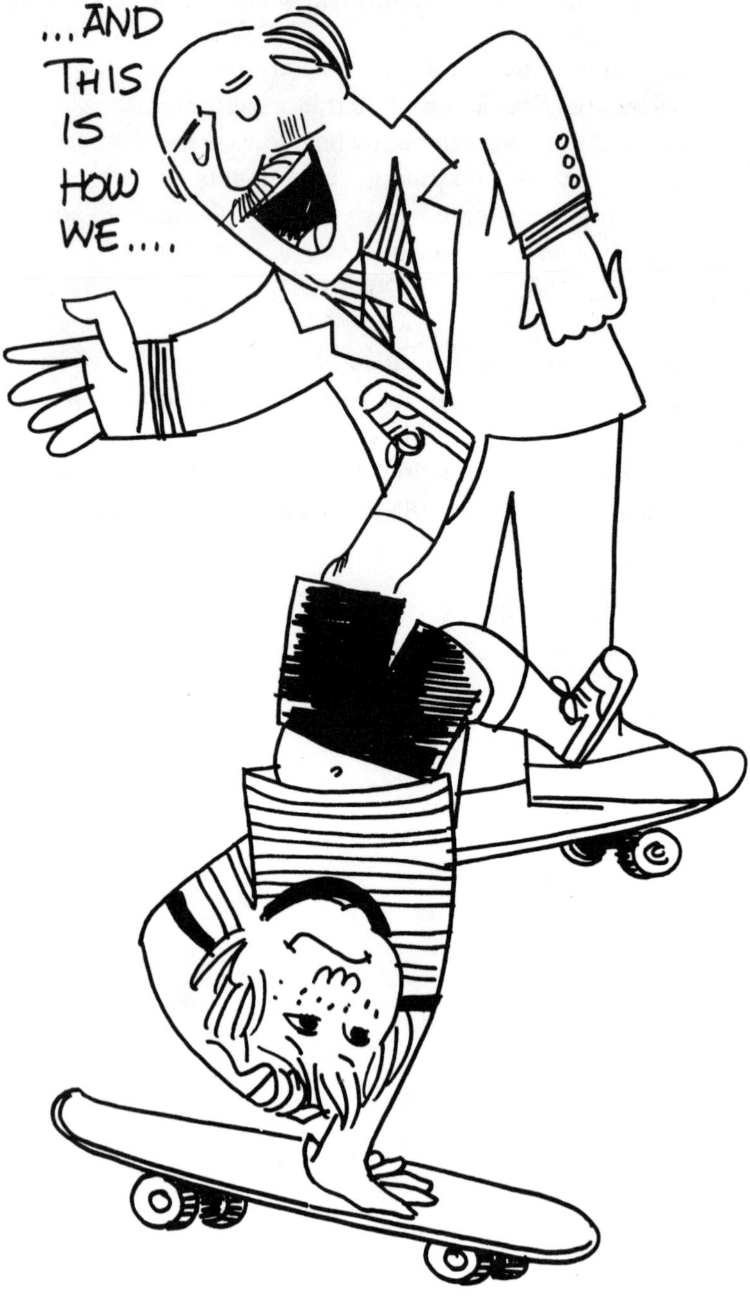
...AND THIS IS HOW WE....

CHAPTER VII

AM I A CUPFILLER OR A CANDLELIGHTER?

A simple definition of a cupfiller is a person who, consciously or unconsiously, goes through life filling or attempting to fill other people's cups with his knowledge, wisdom and experience. A candlelighter, on the other hand, is a person who sees other people as having an individual and unique candle. The candlelighter goes through life lighting others' candles or "turning them on" to their individuality, their uniqueness, to themselves. A cupfiller wants others to be just like him or her. A candlelighter wants others to be themselves.

My experience has been that there are more cupfillers than candlelighters. Many parents want their children to live up to their blueprint of a good boy or good girl. Many principals want their teachers to follow their "game plan" of the "good teacher." There are far too many bosses insisting on only their idea of the "perfect worker." Many husbands and wives want their spouse to follow their blueprint alone.

Perhaps this flows logically from the fact that we are a role conscious and role oriented society. We automatically create expectations or roles for the people that enter our lives.

BASIC BELIEFS OF A CUPFILLER

Our beliefs and our basic values determine, to a great extent, the way we act toward other people. The following are some essential beliefs of the "thoroughbred" cupfiller:

1. If others are left to themselves, they will "goof" and turn out badly.

2. Others need to be closely watched, guided, and supervised.

3. If you let others make their own decisions, they will make the wrong ones.

4. Safeguard others from making mistakes. You learned the hard way and you don't want them to go through what you went through.

METHODS OF A CUPFILLER

Basic to all of these methods is the fact that they are not communication, they are communiques. Communication is a two-way street. Communiques are a oneway street, e.g., from the cupfiller to the "cupfillee" (the one whose cup he is filling). The cupfiller is usually unaware of how the person who is receiving his communiques really feels. He is so obsessed with his sacred responsibility to keep his subject on the "straight and narrow" that he never takes time to listen how the person being kept on the "straight and narrow" path feels about it.

How does the cupfiller go about filling others' cups? He simply makes use of the following tried and true methods.

1. Orders
Ordering is a very common method. "Johnnie, be quiet in class and respect your teacher," a mother tells her son. However, respect is an attitude and it is impossible to order an attitude change. Respect in the real meaning is something that has to be earned by

the person and can't be commanded. Actually, the teacher must have so much going for her that Johnnie really thinks she is "neat." It could be that she may have hardly anything going for her, in fact, she could be a real loser. If so, she's going to have a hard time getting Johnnie's respect no matter how often he hears the command: "Respect your teacher!" Often, ordering doesn't work. It well may have the reverse effect. Johnnie may be feeling 'I'm really not capable of doing much on my own because everyone is always telling me what to do."

2. Threat

Threat is a method often used. One fire chief was notorious for his threat approach. He was always threatening extra work, extra duty to firemen not conforming to his multitude of rules (many more than the Ten Commandments). Threat may get things done but it has a lot of unhealthy fallout. One major defect is a high level of hostility it produces. "I hate the Chief's guts!" was a common saying among the firemen. Hostility usually generates an attitude of "getting even." The Chief's threats actually created a very poor working climate, e.g., one of animosity and revenge.

One time at a big fire, the Chief got there first and in his excitement (he usually "lost his cool" at a fire), parked his car right in front of the fire plug. When the pumper-engine arrived to hook up the plug, the men recognized the Chief's car blocking off the fire plug. Instead of trying to move the car, they immediately opened the two front doors and laid the hose through the front seat. This was a safe way of getting even and embarrassing the Chief.

3. Moralizing

Moralizing is also a very common tool used even by the sincerest parents who really want the best for their children. "Now listen, Billy, I went through life with no college education and it was during the depression years. I really suffered; I don't want you to go through it. If you don't go to college, you are going to end up low man on the totem pole in life."

Moralizing, though sincere, has reverse effects at times. In the case of Billy, it seems he has two choices: agree with Dad or end up "low man on the totem pole," at least in his Dad's eyes. Maybe Billy loves mechanics, working with his hands and dislikes a white collar job. Moralizing could push him into a career of unhappiness or low level satisfaction because he was afraid to displease his parents.

I have had a number of people tell me: "I really never did want to do this kind of work. I went into this field to please my parents." The basic question is: Which is more important . . . being you or pleasing your parents?

4. Blaming or Judging

Blaming, judging or criticizing are common tools when the cupfiller runs head-on into a value system different from his own. "How could you tell a story like that to the women of the Altar & Rosary Society? What are they going to think about the priests of this parish? Don't you ever think before you act?" shouted the pastor to his young assistant. To the young priest, telling the mildly off-colored story was perfectly acceptable. To the pastor it didn't fit the role of a cleric.

The young priest kept on telling his stories. He just didn't let the pastor in on what he was doing. This is often the result of blaming or judging. It really doesn't change values. All it does is to drive the person underground. He just doesn't express his value system when the "boss" is around.

5. Ridiculing
Some cupfillers love to ridicule. "Putting others down" seems to be their favorite in-door sport. It gives them the sense of being superior, above others. An angry mother is upset when she finds out that her son was missing school. "Go ahead, Edward, play hookey from school! Get kicked out! Grow up and be an idiot like your father; see if I give a damn," fumes Mom. She gets in a "double whammie"; she gets both the son and the father with one punch but is completely unaware of the fringe "benefits" from her use of ridicule. First of all, Eddie feels put down. He feels a little more "not okay." He happens to like his Dad who was a high school dropout and holds down a menial job. He really resents his mother calling his Dad an idiot. Another spinoff from ridicule is that he has learned to dislike his formal name EDWARD. He cringes every time someone calls his name. Why? Every time his Mom would start out her verbal spanking, she used his full name. Even though the mother's intention was sincere, her method makes Eddie grow in his belief that he doesn't have much worth, that he is not okay. I personally feel, along with self-concept psychologists, that people who feel they are not okay, act accordingly.

6. Interpreting
Interpreting is sort of a "sly" skill which the cupfiller uses when he is confronted with another's value sys-

tem that doesn't fit into his own. Because interpreting is a "cover-up" method, it is somewhat more difficult for people to be aware of it.

Not too long ago I was having coffee with a person who had recently been divorced after twenty-three years of marriage. I'll never forget him saying, "As I look back, the one thing that really bugged me in my marriage was the fact that she would never accept how I really felt. Every time I expressed my feelings she would answer, 'Oh, now dear, you really don't feel that way, do you?'" This is a classic example of interpretation. His wife could not accept his real feelings, so she changed them to fit into what was acceptable. Her image of a good husband just didn't take in certain feelings. When he came up with feelings that didn't fit the role of a husband, she interpreted the feelings to make them fit the role.

Needless to say, this didn't increase love, belonging or communication in the marriage. In fact, it could very well have been a major cause of its breakdown since lack of communication is (according to some studies) the number one cause of marriage breakdown.

A major result of interpreting is the fact that the other person never really feels that they are really being heard. Often, when a person feels not listened to, he feels he isn't being accepted. Not being accepted is one of the stepping stones to the feeling of "I'm not okay" because I have to act contrary to my feelings to be accepted. Interpretation encourages people to be "phonies." Being a phony is far from being a healthy personality and a long way from having fun being yourself.

7. Analyzing

The "thoroughbred" cupfiller uses the tool of analysis almost automatically. Consciously or unconsciously, he feels he has arrived. He sits back in the ivory tower of his value system and attempts to determine what will be best for others so they can reach "the good life." This is exemplified by the supervisor who calls a secretary in for a talk. "Joan, I've been thinking about you. After analyzing your work record, I noticed you always worked for smaller offices. You no doubt prefer small offices."

The supervisor who is analyzing has the best intentions in the world. Good intentions alone, however, are not enough. Communication means being aware of how your words are affecting the other person. The cupfiller doesn't have this awareness. As a result, a lot of unplanned-for results happen.

First of all, Joan resents the "Father knows best" approach which she sees in her supervisor. Secondly, she feels "put down" literally and utterly detests being analyzed. She feels left out because she had no share in any of the plans. On top of all this, she knows that the poor supervisor is way out in left field because she really prefers large offices to small ones. She grew up in a small town where everyone knew everyone's every move. She learned to appreciate her privacy; she likes large offices and big cities. The real truth of the matter, she seems "out of it" because she has been going through a divorce which has been traumatic. The cupfiller with all his high level ability has struck out again.

8. Probing or Questioning
Things didn't go right for Mr. Coyle, the math teacher.

Some smart aleck kids put a tack on his chair. Luckily he discovered it before sitting down. Putting tacks on teachers' chairs is entirely opposed to his values; many, I'm sure, would agree with him. The way he goes about getting to the bottom of the case is open to question.

He publicly begins to ask those whom he suspects. They all deny putting the tack on his chair. He announces that they will stay after school until someone confesses. He calls a good reliable student, Mark, to his desk. "Mark, who did it?" he asks. Mark happens to have a different set of values. He needs a sense of belonging with his peers. If he were to "snitch," he could certainly lose that. Mark's only out is to lie: "Sorry, Mr. Coyle, I was working on the problems and didn't see anything." Mr. Coyle is upset and wants to get even with the culprit. Another word for this is that he wants revenge because someone dared violate his value system. He is geared for his regular win-lose battle and he always wins because he can flunk the "no good" students, as he calls them.

Mr. Coyle thinks he is inculcating the right values. He sends only communiques and finds it hard to communicate with the students. He is totally unaware of the effects of his probing approach. The 24 students who were kept after school feel they are getting an unfair deal and resent it. The good students were put on the spot and had to lie to keep their sense of belonging with the gang. The kid who finally admitted everything two weeks later joined the thousands of drop-outs . . . actually became a member of the "push-outs." Those pushed out by teachers like Mr. Coyle. Could Mr. Coyle have approached it differently? Might not the tack have been taken as a warning that his approach to students was creating hostility and the kids were retaliating? Taken in this light, he could have examined his way of dealing with students. However, being a dyed-in-the-wool cupfiller, he felt that he had the "right values." If you figure you've arrived, then there is no place to go. So, unfortunately, the "arrived" or the "perfect" Mr. Coyle was overjoyed to find out that the kid who put the tack on his chair finally dropped out of school. "Glad we got rid of the kid!" he joyously muttered in the faculty lounge.

9. Diverting
Diverting is another skill used by the cupfiller who finds it difficult to accept things that are a threat to his or her basic value system. For instance, take the case of Dorothy. One of her values is that complaining is a sign of weakness. Her Dad never complained, he always rolled with the punches. She likes to believe that Joe, her husband, has the same "roll with the punches" value also.

Joe comes home from work one evening upset and depressed. He begins to talk about the run-in he had with the boss. Quickly, Dorothy fixes him up with a drink and says: "Honey, have a drink and read the paper. You'll forget all about it." Again she successfully helped Joe roll with the punches by diverting his mind from his problem.

What she doesn't realize is that the problem remains. Joe just represses it because he has a wife that cannot listen when she hears anything contrary or upsetting. Instead of helping Joe by listening, she helped him to repress it. Repression has diminished Joe's happiness as well as given him a non-acceptance feeling from his wife. She cannot accept him when he can't roll with the punches like "Dear Old Dad" used to do.

A CUPFILLER SUMMED UP

A cupfiller creates a gap between himself and the person whose cup he is filling. It turns out to be a role-to-role or "follower-leader" relationship. It more often than not is a "put down" to the person whose cup is being filled. Although the cupfiller's intentions may be honorable, the effect of his cupfilling is often a psychological ripoff. Some of the messages people receive from a cupfiller are: "He doesn't feel I am capable of making my own decision," or "He thinks I'm helpless," or "I want to be me and not another him," or "He thinks I'm not okay," or "Someday I'll get even." The cupfiller approach tends to reduce rather than build up the psychological size or the okay feeling of the other person.

As a counselor in three different high schools and talking to literally hundreds of teenagers, I learned that many of their parents were sincere cupfillers. The one most common complaint was "My parents won't let me be myself. They want to make me into their image and likeness." I also worked with a lot of kids on drugs. One of the most common reasons these kids gave for using drugs was to escape the pressure of their parents and relations, the pressure to mold them into their idea of a 'good boy' or 'good girl.' This is exemplified by the mother who said to me: "My children are like clay and my duty is to mold them into good boys." The sad thing is that she had a very restrictive idea of what it means to be a good kid. Her kid could be good, but if he didn't "jive" with her idea of good, he would get a "rejected feeling" from his mother.

I really feel that if some parents were God, there would be only one flower. "Now this is my idea of a good flower," the parent would say. Thank God that the Creator has a much broader outlook. As a result, we have a whole variety of flowers from orchids to lillies. If a cupfiller parent could be more like God, they would widen their concept of the "good" boy, "good" girl to allow room for their children to be good by being themselves instead of playing a role to please their parents.

Will I ever forget the boy in high school who played in a Rock & Roll band? Naturally he had long hair (short hair in such a band was not the "in thing" for the "now" generation!). However, his mother could not see how her Bobby could be a good boy and have long hair. Every morning without fail he could hear her ridicule and nagging, "Get that hair cut and join the human race again." His only way of coping, he told me, was to go on drugs. I am sure his mother did not have drugs in her concept of a "good" boy, but the use of the cupfiller approach often brings about unexpected results.

BASIC BELIEFS OF A CANDLELIGHTER

The candlelighter's beliefs are quite different from the beliefs of the cupfiller. His communication with people is so different because his concept of human nature is different from the cupfiller.

1. Others are basically good. Given the proper atmosphere people will turn out "real good."

2. Delegation and trust are essential to help people attain worth and dignity.

3. Freedom is one of man's greatest possessions. The candlelighter creates climates whereby people can make choices by giving them dignity and self-respect.

4. Allows others to make mistakes. Experimental knowledge is an essential means of growing.

5. Self-knowledge is the key to a healthy personality. As a person sees himself, so he acts. If he sees himself as a worthless person, he acts in a worthless way. A person grows in proportion to how well he sees the worth and dignity he has as a unique person.

6. The greatest treasure anyone can offer this world is the uniqueness of his or her person; for there never was or never will be another person just like themselves.

7. Seeks a common union with others by emphasizing those things that unite rather than those which divide.

8. Being a "good" boy, "good" teacher, "good" secretary or anything, is best accomplished by being yourself. You can't really be "good" for anyone else unless you feel "good" about yourself as a person.

PRINCIPLE METHODS OF A CANDLELIGHTER

The principle method of the candlelighter is the ability to break out of the role-to-role relationship (boss-worker; teacher-pupil) and create a 1-to-1 or person-to-person relationship. A candlelighter realizes that no growth takes place for anyone in a role-to-role relationship. He is open to growth as a person and creates an accepting atmosphere in which others can grow. The ability to break through roles to create a person-to-person relationship is the hallmark of the candlelighter. The real candlelighter has reached the stage of "Having fun being himself." The major method of doing this must include effective listening and communication.

I KNOW A CANDLELIGHTER

There are three boys in my family. My Dad was a "Santa Claus," a really kind person who was gone half the time because he worked on the 24 hours on and 24 hours off shifts of the Fire Department. Mom was there every day and she was a "thoroughbred" candlelighter. She gave us freedom of choice with plenty of room to try various things. In an atmosphere of love and acceptance I was able to be myself. I learned to value freedom highly in this atmosphere. Presently, I am working for myself and getting paid for my hobby (communicating with people). I really enjoy doing what I am doing. More than likely, I wouldn't be in this ideal position if I had had a cupfiller instead of a candlelighter for a Mother.

HOW ARE YOU MISS WINSOME?
NOT SO GOOD TODAY, MR. DUDD. MY MOTHER BROKE HER HIP... MY SON IS FAILING IN SCHOOL ... MY HUSBAND HAS DESERTED US... THE I.R.S.
... FINE, FINE GLAD TO HEAR IT! COULD YOU GET THE REPORT TO ME TODAY?

CHAPTER VIII

CAN I COMMUNICATE THROUGH LISTENING?

or

(How to Become a Candlelighter Through Effective Listening)

In marriage, at school, in business and on the streets a lot of talk goes on, tons of communiques are sent but it's been my experience that little communication takes place. This is understandable if we remember that we are in a role oriented society. Role playing means unequal psychological size!

Psychological undersize means one person doesn't feel on an equal plane with the other. A student may be reluctant to say what he feels if he thinks the teacher is wiser and smarter than himself in all walks of life. A worker may be afraid to say what he feels to his boss because his boss has more power than he has. As a result, there is not a communication relationship but a communique relationship.

JUST WHAT IS COMMUNICATION

Actually, there is, perhaps, no word more misunderstood in America than *communication*. The person who can talk and tell jokes is not necessarily a communicator. Someone who is very articulate or even someone who has been "vaccinated with a phonograph needle" and is forever talking doesn't necesssarily communicate. The common belief that talking means communicating is a myth that confuses people. To really understand what communication means we have to go back to the Latin word from which it came. (I studied Latin 8 years. When I finished, the Catholic Church switched to English.) The root word in Latin means *common union*. The very basic and essential meaning of communication, then, is the *ability to create a common union with the person and with the other person or persons with whom you are talking.*

MANY COMMUNICATION EXPERTS CAN'T COMMUNICATE

Sounds like a contradiction? Yes, it is . . . unfortunately. Not too long ago a good friend and I had a business lunch with an "expert" in training business and industry people in communication. He told us what he did, the new ideas he was working on, what projects he intended to make in five years, etc. etc. In fact he was hogging the conversation about 90% of the time; he wasn't communicating with me or my friend in the true (Latin) sense of the word. What he unconsciously was doing was telling us how effective he was in his role of trainer in communications. It really seems this expert was creating a role-to-role relationship. As a result, his conversation was not communication, but communiques. Role-to-role relationships are always communiques. 1-to-1 or person-to-person relationships are necessary before real communication can take place. One of the sure signs that our communication "expert" could not communicate was the fact that he was so busy telling us what he does, how he does it, and how much he was going to make that he left little or no time to listen to what we may have had to say.

However, I really was not surprised to find a communication "expert" who could talk, but not communicate. In 1967 and 1968 I went to every "high level" communication workshop I could. The workshops had a low batting average. About 30% were effective; the other 70% I placed in the talking but not communicating category. I found a lot of "cupfillers" who believed they had arrived and were going to make you just like them. This was especially true in a lot of the poor sensitivity training that was popular in those years. At the time, I couldn't pin-point just why these "experts" weren't communicating. It was only when I studied the basic meaning of the word 'communicate' that I understood why many people then, as well as today, talk a lot but communicate little or not at all in their workshops.

HOW DO YOU CREATE A COMMON UNION?

First, you have to be aware that we are in a role oriented society. If you have a college degree, the non-college graduate may look upon you as smarter by far. So you have an automatic difference in psychological size.

UNEQUAL PSYCHOLOGICAL SIZE = COMMUNIQUE

COLLEGE GRAD

NON - COLLEGE GRAD

The person who has no degree may be much more intelligent than you are. However, he feels beneath you and therefore his psychological size is unequal to yours. How do you equalize size or create a common union?

A COMMON UNION = COMMUNICATION

It is not enough to say that I don't feel above the person just because he doesn't have a degree. The essential point to remember is how does the *other* person feel. If he or she feels below you, you do not have a common union. What then, is the way to create a common union?

EFFECTIVE LISTENING—THE KEY TO COMMON UNION

In our culture this seems to be a contradiction. Usually, we picture the communicator as the talker, joke-teller, disc jockey type; the listener as the quiet, accepting person who says little, but listens a lot. In fact, often the listener chooses that way because he feels he hasn't got much worthwhile to say, but at least he can listen. This is the passive listener.

The listener that communicates or creates the common union through listening is the ACTIVE listener. He or she has acquired the difficult art of listening or the art of creating a common union with other people, the art of communication in the true sense of the word. Two essential elements make up this area of communicating through listening. One is a set of attitudes, the other is a set of skills. Put them together and you have a person who is a first class communicator . . . the *active* listener.

ESSENTIAL ATTITUDES FOR EFFECTIVE LISTENING

All the active listening skills in the world are totally ineffective without basic attitudes. Attitudes are to the skills what gasoline is to the car. The car won't go without gas no matter how costly the model. A person cannot effectively listen without the right attitudes. The following attitudes are what I consider to be essential:

1. Caring or Concern
To be an effective listener, you have to really be interested and concerned with other persons. You have to be concerned with how they feel. Note well, you can't fake it for long. One father read a book in which

he learned that he should be interested in his children's point of view. So he let them express their viewpoints and then told them exactly what they were expected to do . . . if they wanted to live in his house. He was a cupfiller, no doubt about it. Cupfillers' attitudes just won't make it in effective listening.

2. Assumption of Worth

The effective listener assumes that the other person has worth and a lot to offer. This flows from the basic assumption about human nature. Human beings, given proper climate, will turn out "real good." The active listener assumes that "goodness" is in the other person. Moreover, his attitude that the other person is worthwhile helps the other see himself as worthwhile.

This is what is called the self-fulfilling prophecy. If we look at others as worthwhile, it helps them feel worthwhile. If we look at others as "not okay," it helps them feel "not okay." In other words, one's self concept (how he sees himself) is influenced by how others see him, especially significant others, i.e. parents, teachers, friends.

3. Acceptance

This quality is what truly divides the cupfiller from the candlelighter. The cupfiller assumes he has arrived and has the right value system. He cannot accept anyone with a different set of values. The candlelighter assumes that everyone is unique and no one fits into a mold. Because he assumes that people can be different and have different values and still be worthwhile, it is easy for him to accept others. In fact, he welcomes differences. The fact that everyone is different, that everyone has a different candle is what makes life so "alive" for the candlelighter.

A classic example of how the lack of acceptance makes effective listening impossible comes from one fire department. Three fire chiefs from different states were on the oral examinations board for Lieutenant Examination. It was well known that one candidate was extremely qualified and orals were but a formality. However, the candidate came to the orals wearing lighter blue stockings rather than the dark uniformed ones. One of the examiners, an apparent cupfiller, hardly listened to what the candidate said but zeroed in on the breach of uniform regulation. He marked the young man low because he did not fit into his idea of what values an officer should have. As a result, the best man did not get the job.

4. Empathy
Empathy is the ability to see the world as the other person sees it. We all know that a small child views life much differently than an adult. His experience is limited, he's working from a younger, untried mind. Most adults recognize the fact and make allowances for it, having empathy with the small child's world view. But, really, each adult has a different background, various but limited experience and untried abilities so that empathy, the ability to experience the world as the other experiences it, is as important to other adults as it is for small children. The candle-

lighter's motto can be taken from the Indian proverb: "Don't judge another until you've walked one mile in his moccasins!"

5. *The* **Desire** *to Learn from Everyone You Meet.*
If you have the desire to learn from everyone you meet, it means you are assuming that everyone you meet has something to offer. If you acquire this attitude, your whole life becomes a beautiful learning experience. If you have this attitude plus the learned skills of effective listening, your life will be extremely enriched.

I added this qualification because it was something I learned from personal experience from the Hawaiian teenagers. In 1959 I was assigned to a parish in Honolulu as assistant pastor, director of youth, and school counselor. Before I got there the youth club was at a standstill. I was going to liven it up. I was young, I had had a lot of super experiences when I was a teenager, I thought I could relate well to teenagers. I got several parents together and we decided to start monthly dances. It was a disaster. Month after month we could get only about 20 teenagers to come. I would say to the parent chaperons, "Well, when I was a teenager, all my friends would be at a dance like this." I was actually ready to throw in the towel and call it quits; the kids of today just don't appreciate things like the good old days. I didn't realize it, but I was a first-class cupfiller. With all my experience, my degrees in education, I was going to help these teenagers experience the "good life." Actually I was playing the "Big Daddy," the "good father" and they were the "little children." I related well to the teenagers; I could talk to them, but I was not communicating with them. I was decreasing their psychological size while

"BIG DADDY"

HAWAIIAN TEENAGERS

increasing mine. At this time, however, I knew nothing about the theory of communication or the concepts of psychological size. Luckily, I didn't give up. Instead, I selected six "on the ball" teenagers and formed a committee. I really didn't admit I had flopped in the dance program. I did, however, ask them for suggestions to make a more successful program. Unknowingly, I made my first step toward creating a common union with these teenagers. Instead of having things done for them, they now were part of the planning board with a share in the action. They were doing things for themselves and for other teenagers. They felt a sense of worth and dignity which I had unintentionally robbed them of by being "Big Daddy."

What happened when I made the switch from a cup-filler to a candlelighter? The results were unbelievable. From that group of six teenagers grew 14 different clubs of teenagers. The dance club alone was soon averaging a thousand teenagers a dance instead of the usual 20. The sports club created a huge sports league with more members than the parochial league in the city. High school students were coaching little kids in the intramurals, using sports as a means to develop cooperation and sportsmanship. These teenagers were expanding and growing. They felt worthwhile because they were doing worthwhile things. They sold Christmas trees, operated an ice cream shop and other business ventures to finance their helping clubs, social clubs, hospital clubs, etc.

The clubs and their varied activities received a good deal of press coverage. Teachers from one of the other islands in the Hawaiian group asked me over to explain the thriving sports league. As a former cupfiller, I would have gone over without a second thought. But as a recent candlelighter convert, I asked the President of the sports league, a teenager, if she would do it. She felt thrilled. She flew to Maui, talked to all the teachers, and after a few weeks Maui had their own program going full swing.

I sat back and watched one candle being lit after another, one club being born after another, until the combined youth clubs exceeded 1500 teenagers not to count the many more thousands in elementary schools coached and helped by the teenagers.

I had a classmate, a missionary in the Solomon Islands, who was working with quite poor, primitive people. They desperately needed a hospital. The crowning achievement of the new "Candlelighter" teenage club was that they accepted the challenge to help the people in the Solomon Islands build their own hospital. In less than ten years they sent over $13,000 for the hospital which has been in full operation since 1969. It is named Star of the Sea Hospital after the teenagers from the parish of the same name who helped build it. Paper work, bookkeeping and records of the vast number of clubs was taken care of by the Secretary Club made up of twenty secretaries under the direction of their teacher, Sr. Florence Louise who really worked her heart out together with the other Sisters of Notre Dame.

To sum it up, I went to teach something to the Hawaiian teenagers. I learned much much more than what I had to teach. I learned the desire to learn from everyone. I learned that being a cupfiller was a "drag" and switching to a candlelighter has been one of the most rewarding switch-overs I've ever made.

ESSENTIAL SKILLS FOR EFFECTIVE LISTENING

The skills needed rests on a simple awareness that people speak on two channels, the channel of their words and the channel of their feelings.

1. Listening for Feeling (Channel 5)

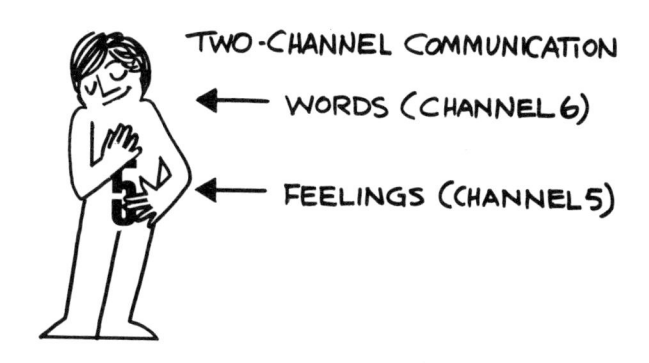

TWO-CHANNEL COMMUNICATION

← WORDS (CHANNEL 6)

← FEELINGS (CHANNEL 5)

TWO CHANNEL COMMUNICATION

We can never fully listen to someone unless we can tune in on both channels, which are always in operation. We have to be *aware* of the feelings channel, then try to *listen* for their feelings. It requires some practice, but with effort it can be done. The following is a little test to try on yourself. I use it in my government class on Listening & Memory Improvement. See if you can go through it and pick up the feeling behind the words of each sentence.

Self-Test for Listening Skills

Example:
Person Says:
"I can't figure it out. Maybe I should just throw in the towel."

Person is Feeling:
a) stumped
b) give-up

Person says:
1. Just think, three more days, and I will be GS 6.

2. Wow, I finished the whole three page letter without a mistake.

3. My husband got that big job, but it looks like we will have to move.

4. I don't mind the class, but I have heard it all before.

5. My new boss thinks I am two people. I don't know how I'll ever get the work done.

6. It is a changing world. All my friends moved. I have to drink coffee alone now.

7. Working for him is like working for Hitler.

8. Do you think R.I.F. will hit our office?

9. I've never lost an argument in my life.

10. She thinks she is God's gift to the world.

11. I work a full day in the office just like you, Dear, how about helping with dishes.

12. My new job pays well, but I don't know a person in the office.

13. Our office was the best in the agency until Lulabelle transferred in.

14. Talking to my spouse is like talking to myself.

15. What am I going to do when I retire?

HOW WELL DID YOU DO?

The following is really step one, i.e., to be able to determine what was the feeling behind the person's words. Here are the answers to the FEELING TEST.

Person is Feeling:
 1. Achievement, happiness
 2. Accomplishment
 3. Mixed feelings; happiness, disappointment
 4. Boredom
 5. Over-burdened
 6. Lonely
 7. Dominated
 8. Anxiety
 9. Confidence
 10. Resentment
 11. Cheated
 12. Lonely
 13. Dislike
 14. Frustrated
 15. Worry

2. Listening **is** *Speaking*

Another apparent contradiction? Actually, to listen actively you *must* speak. It simply means that effective listening is a very active listening. First, you actively listen for feelings, then you actually respond in words to these feelings to check out with the person your understanding of those feelings. Listening is not the passive nodding of the head or slight clucking sounds of approval, but the active exploring of what another is saying and feeling. To demonstrate active listening let us take the first few questions on the feeling test.

Number 1 was: "Just think, three more days and I will be a GS 6." A response of an active listener would be: "You must really feel a sense of accomplishment." If you have hit on their feeling accurately, the person will respond: "Boy, you said it. I had to go to school nights to get to this level." One feeling leads to another and soon you find yourself engaged in significant communication. You have succeeded in understanding the other person. You have communicated to him that he has worth as a person. In other words, you have created a common union.

Instead of actively listening, you could respond in more conventional ways; e.g., "I know what you mean. I had a struggle to make my last promotion. You know I had to . . etc." In this case you have switched the focus of attention to yourself, a most common cocktail party skill. Still another response could have been: "It's about time you made a GS 6." This is, of course, a "put down." It is the opposite of creating a common union. It creates more separation.

In 1968, I learned this active listening skill in the course "The Techniques of Counseling" by Dr. Bill

Sease of Colorado University, a person who really could create a common union with people. Since then, I've taken it up as my hobby. I have found that physical starvation has its counterpart . . . psychological starvation. While millions of people in the underdeveloped world are slowly dying from lack of food, many more are drying up in the developed worlds from a lack of feelings-recognition. People are starving to be listened to, to be heard. For me it has been a key to sharing people's fears and disappointments as well as hopes and dreams.

I'll never forget the young man who was returning his little daughter to his former wife. She was too young to fly alone, so he had to bring her back. I listened to how he felt about his divorce, how it hit his self-concept, how cautious he was in terms of being re-married. For an hour and a half he shared his life and his feelings as a divorced man. When we arrived in Montana, before getting off the plane, he said: "Jim I have two hours before I fly back. How about continuing our talk at lunch?" The interest of a perfect stranger had triggered off something inside him. He was suffering from an advanced case of psychological hunger. This hunger was satisfied through active listening.

THE EFFECTS OF ACTIVE LISTENING

Learning active listening is a challenging task. It demands the ability to be open minded to different values; it requires the ability to see things from the other person's world and the empathy to feel how the other feels. In my opinion, however, the beautiful effects far outweigh the work involved to acquire these skills. Some of the major effects are the following:

1. *Listening can enhance self-concept* . . . true listening assumes the other person has worth, dignity, and something to offer and this attitude makes the other person feel good about himself.

2. *Listening may solve the problem for the other person* . . . giving a person a chance to talk through his problem may clarify his thinking about the subject as well as provide the necessary emotional release.

3. *Listening can reduce tension* . . . giving the other person a chance to get his problem or viewpoint off his chest may help to "clear the air" of tension and hostility.

4. *Listening facilitates cooperation* . . . when a person feels that you are really interested in him and his problems, thought, and opinions, he respects you and will more readily cooperate with you.

5. *Listening promotes "common union" communication* . . . in marriage, in schools, in the business world communication is essential for happy relations. Often, communication breaks down because neither party has learned to listen. Skillful listening has solved many communication problems — because of its powerful effect of equalizing psychological size.

6. *Listening can help you grow* . . . sharing in the values and beliefs of another person can help you grow in your values and beliefs as well as developing open attitudes — a basic condition of growth.

7. *Listening can win friends* . . . a person can't help appreciating you for attentively listening to his feelings. (This is important for children who desire to learn how to make friends.)

8. *Listening can deepen relationships* . . . listening to each other's real feelings is one of the most effective ways to deepen a relationship between friends or between husband and wife. Communication on a depth level cannot take place without active listening.

9. *Listening develops an active mind* . . . real listening is active. The listener is continually trying to understand the feelings behind the words of the speaker. He tries to feel those feelings, to see the world through the speaker's eyes.

10. *Listening is enjoyable* . . . because it is challenging, enriching, adventuresome. It is absolutely essential to reach the stage of "Having Fun Being Yourself"!

INTELLECTUAL LISTENING

There is another side to listening, listening to ideas. I put the "active" or feeling listening first because I feel that it is a more important tool to reach the goal of "Having Fun Being Yourself." Intellectual or idea listening is also quite important.

THE NEED IS CLEAR

When studies indicated that 45% of the average working day of the ordinary person was spent in listening, educators became aware of the need to improve listening. Other studies indicated that college freshmen listened only at a 25% effectiveness level. From all this came an incredible awareness that schools from K through college had no class on *how* to listen. Although some colleges have some today, hardly any elementary or secondary schools have listening courses. Studies in business pointed out that in some of the major businesses listening effectiveness came out at a 20% effective rate.

I have been teaching this type of course for the Civil Service Training Center. In giving this course again and again I have had people say: "Jim, in my work, communication and listening are essential. I have spent years in school from kindergarden through college and never once came up with a course on listening." This book is written to help fulfill the education gap which unfortunately still exists.

QUALITIES OF A GOOD LISTENER

Maybe you would like to see where you stand in terms of essential qualities of the good listener? These characteristics, actually, flow from attitudes.

1. Freshness of Appreciation
The good listener is never bored because he is interested in everything. Unlike the poor listener who, being acquainted with the topic, thinks he has heard it all before, the good listener will try to learn something new from a topic even if he is really up on the subject.

2. Goes beyond Speaker to the Message
The good listener is not thrown off balance because he doesn't like the way the speaker looks or talks. The poor listener, on the contrary, is upset by minor considerations. A good example is at a speech where

the Poor Listener says: "Look at the length of his hair! No hippie is going to tell me anything." Long hair, short hair, or no hair, it makes little difference to the good listener. He is willing to learn from everyone.

3. The Good Listener has Emotional Control

The good listener listens openly when the speaker presents ideas totally opposed to his own. The poor listener stops listening once he hears something he doesn't agree with. He is completely "bent out of shape" and from that time on, he is preparing an answer instead of listening to what the other person is saying.

4. The Good Listener Listens for Central Ideas

He sees facts only in as much as they fit in with the principle idea. The poor listener, however, writes down one fact after another. Afterwards he has a collection of facts that are comparable to a jig-saw puzzle. He just can't put it all together.

5. The Good Listener Actively Tries to Get Involved with the Speaker's Ideas

He anticipates what is going to be said. He relates it to things he already knows. The poor listener fakes attention. He may be in class looking directly at the teacher but his mind is deciding which of the girls he should be taking to the dance. He's not there in mind though his body is in class.

6. Needs a Challenge

The good listener will not avoid a topic simply because it seems too difficult. He will tackle anything.

He needs a challenge to keep himself intellectually alive. The poor listener avoids a challenge. In college he will drop out of the difficult classes and look for the "fresh air" courses. Studies have found out that the good listener among college students prefers the experience of programs as "Face the Nation," "Town Meeting" and other challenging 'idea' programs. The poor listener hardly ever tunes in on programs deeper than the situation comedies or "Gunsmoke." In other words, the poor listener has a history of avoiding challenging ideas programs while the good listener accepts the challenging ones.

7. The Good Listener is Interested in Others

The good listener is interested in other people and therefore interested in what they have to say. The poor listener seems to be overconcerned with himself. He seems to be so concerned with his world that he hasn't much room for the ideas which interest others.

8. The Good Listener Uses His Free Time Well

Many people are not aware of the "free time" in listening. The average person talks at the rate of 125 words per minute. (Some exceptional people's rate is 200 with gusts up to 275.) Before an audience a good speaker may slow it down to 100 words per minute. But a normal person has the ability to listen and understand 400-500 words per minute. The good listener uses his "free time" in three ways:

   a. He anticipates where the speaker is heading and contrasts and compares it with what he knows already about the subject.

   b. He looks for evidence and examples that support the speaker's main ideas.

c. Every three or four minutes he summarizes in his own mind the main idea or ideas of the speaker. He does this regularly so that he has a continual "instant replay" of what is going on.

The poor listener uses his free time to go on "trips." He is at a football game for a while, then he is with the boys having a drink. He has the ability to create distractions to side-step the challenge of actively listening.

LISTENING **IS** *GROWING*

Growing in the psychological sense means taking in new ideas and experiencing new feelings. Growing to be ourselves is a life-time endeavor. We will never fully reach this unreachable goal, but we can get much closer through the tool of effective listening. Learning to practice "active listening" puts us in touch with the feelings of other people. Being aware of the ideas of others puts us into contact with the ever-changing ideas of others. Being effective on both levels of listening helps us take the big jump toward the goal of "HAVING FUN BEING YOURSELF."

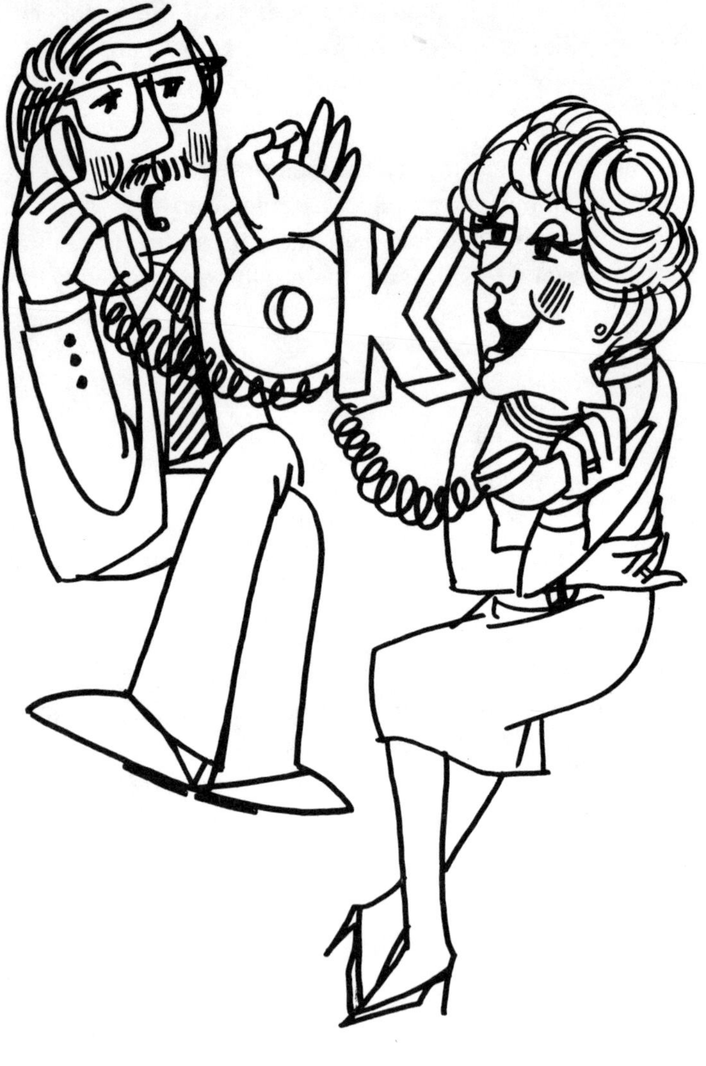
OK

CHAPTER IX

HOW CAN "T.A." HELP ME COMMUNICATE BETTER?

If you are not acquainted with T.A. (Transactional Analysis) you may get a clear picture of it if you see it as a study of the everyday communications (transactions) between people. You may want to read *Born to Win*. You'll probably find it one of the most readable books on the subject.

I look upon T.A. as another approach to being yourself and helping others see themselves as "Okay." I personally like the way it makes use of good everyday language to explain psychological concepts.

INTERIOR T.A.
OR
LISTENING TO YOURSELF

For the sake of clairty, one type of T.A. can be called interior. It assumes that everyone has three kinds of things going on inside of them (ego states): the *parent,* the *adult,* and the *child.* For all practical purposes the *parent* stands for the "should" approach, the *adult* stands for the reasoned approach... "Let's weigh the advantages and disadvantages of this move,"... and the *child* represents the spontaneous "Let's have fun now" approach. This personality model resembles that of Freud in relation to the ego *(adult),* superego *(parent)* and the id *(child).*

Here's an example of a friend of mine called Del that shows what I mean by "Interior T.A." Del loved airplanes. Clearly, he was acting out his *child* because he was never at peace with his decision. He would be flying around Colorado when something inside would say: "Del, you have a wife and five kids to support. You are in no position to have this airplane." (For some this would be called conscience.) In T.A. it is the *parent* saying what should be done.

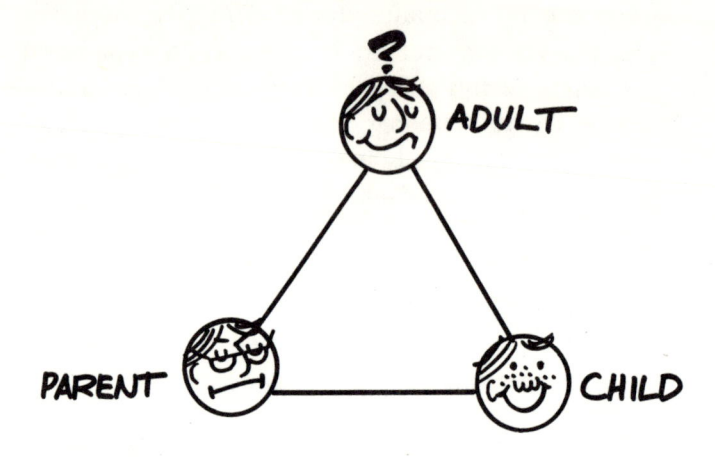

```
              ADULT

  PARENT              CHILD
```

As a result, the *parent* is unhappy, the *child* is happy with the airplane and the *adult* is confused on what to do to keep peace within the personality.

After several months Del, working in his *adult* solved the problem. He sold the airplane which made his *parent* happy and eliminated the nagging. He worked out a deal whereby he could put aside monthly sufficient money for himself, the family and save for a future airplane. His *adult* solved the problem and he was at peace within himself. His *adult* was happy because of the acceptable solution. His *parent* was happy because he got rid of the airplane. His *child* was happy because there is a savings account for a future airplane.

PARENT — *ADULT* — *CHILD*

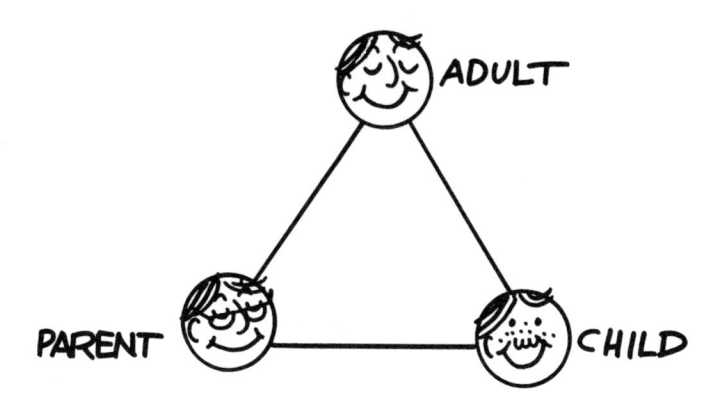

Interior T.A. as I call it, can be a useful tool for listening and understanding yourself better. Try this simple exercise of drawing three circles in the proportion that you see your *parent,* your *adult,* and your *child.* Then draw it again in terms of how you would like to be or how you think others see you. The example below is one taken from a person in my class.

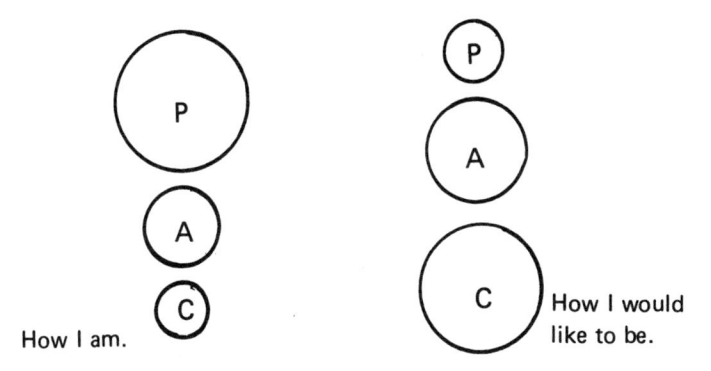

How I am.

How I would like to be.

Notice the difference between how a person is and how this person would like to be. It is an excellent tool for awareness of "who you are and where you would like to go." This person would definitely like to go in the direction of the *child* — more free, more spontaneous, more fun-loving. Knowing where she wants to go is a major step in getting there.

EXTERIOR T.A.
OR
LISTENING TO OTHERS

What I call exterior T.A. is taking a look at and examining your communications (transactions) with people. T.A. is a useful tool to understand how we communicate with people and how we have a chance to communicate more effectively.

I am not giving a thorough coverage of T.A. but picking out some essential ideas that may be helpful to the ordinary person in terms of learning to communicate more effectively. The following illustration points out one of the most common ways people communicate because of our role oriented society.

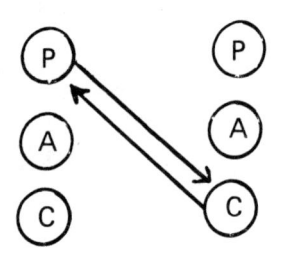

1. Parent-Child Transaction
Much of our so-called "communication" is actually communique because of the difference in psychological size. Moralizing, threatening, interpreting and all the other ways a parent talks to his children are parent-child transactions. The parent who says "Shut up and eat your cereal!" is emphasizing the psychological size between the child and himself. "You are unfair because Johnnie didn't have to eat his!" could well be a typical *child-parent* response to the *parent-child* message.

Some *parent-child* communiques are necessary. Little Johnnie has to be kept from playing with fire because he isn't old enough to realize its danger. However, it seems that *parent-child* communiques are far overused and often with the result that the child gets an "I'm not okay" feeling about himself.

It might surprise some to realize that *parent-child* communiques are often found when adults are talking to one another. "Joe, get that work done or you're not going home tonight!" barks the boss. This clearly is a *parent-child* communique using threat. The boss is the *parent,* Joe is the *child.* Another: Two friends are talking. Bill says, "You'll never get anywhere, Mike, unless you speak up." Bill is sending a *parent-child* communique. Betty says to her husband, "Sam, if you don't finish the grass today, that's all right, but sleep on your side of the bed tonight." The wife's communique is: if you don't do what I say, you will lose your reward.

2. *Adult to Adult Communication*
Here we are back to attitudes. We see ourselves having a common union with the person we are talking to. It is no longer a role-to-role relationship (boss-to-worker, husband-to-wife, etc.); it is an I-to-I or person-to-person. As individual persons, we are both equal and we are both unique so we have something to offer one another. Notice how the transactions become communications instead of communiques. The mother says: "Johnnie, you have the choice between Wheaties or Corn Flakes. Which do you prefer?" The mother is communicating with the *adult* part of Johnnie's personality. He has a good "okay" feeling because his mother respected his feelings and his free will.

"Joe, you're up to your ears in work. Let's figure a way to get it knocked off before quitting time," says the boss. Joe really has a good feeling. Instead of being put down, he feels uplifted because the boss has developed a "common union" by sitting down with him and working out ways of doing the work.

"Honey, I really feel shaggy myself when the grass is so long. I know you have a lot to do, but I sure would be happy if you could find time to cut it," says Betty. Joe responds well to her communication. She recognizes he has a lot to do and doesn't put him down and build up resentment. She is really relating to Joe person-to-person.

TRANSPARENCY & COMMUNICATION

The adult-to-adult communication is really nothing more than the art of being yourself which means the art of being transparent. A classic example is one I use for my communication class for executive secretaries. It is 3:00 in the afternoon. The boss brings in emergency typing that must make it out that day. Molly figures she can do it by 4:30. quitting time. At 4:45 she has to pick up her little boy at school and at 5:00 she has to pick up her husband. She's typing away smoothly and effectively. Perhaps she can just make it under the deadline. Suddenly, Ralph, the office socialite walks over to recount his latest joke. Molly knows any of Ralph's jokes take ten minutes. She continues to type hoping to be able to do two things at once but she "goofs." That's it! She says: "Ralph, can't you see I'm busy? I don't have time for your jokes." He walks away and feels put down. Ralph thought he and Molly had a good relationship but he doubts it now. He feels bad because he was on the receiving end of a parent-child communique.

Actually, Molly could easily switch this communique to communication by being transparent or "congruent" as the psychologists would say.

She could do this in two steps. First, she has to be aware of her feelings, then she has to express them by getting out her frustrations without reducing Ralph's psychological size. Here is what could have happened if she did it this way. When Ralph walked in, Molly would immediately think to herself: "Here comes Ralph. I am sure he is good for a ten minute joke. His jokes are good. I like Ralph, but if I stop now, I'll never make it." Molly is perfectly aware of the situation. When Ralph starts his joke, she stops typing and says: "Ralph, I'd really like to hear your joke but the boss gave me this emergency typing and I have to finish it by 4:30. Right after work I have to pick up my little boy and my husband. Do you mind saving it until tomorrow?" "Okay!" replies Ralph and walks away understandingly admiring Molly's honesty. Molly feels good. She got out her pressures by being transparent. She did it simply by using the first person "I really am under pressure." She avoided the judgmental second person "Can't you see I'm busy." She practices the art of being transparent. She kept and created a deeper common union with Ralph. In T.A. she is communicating on an adult-to-adult level.

Yes, the essential understandable concepts of T.A. could be very helpful in switching the parent-child communiques to the adult-to-adult communication.

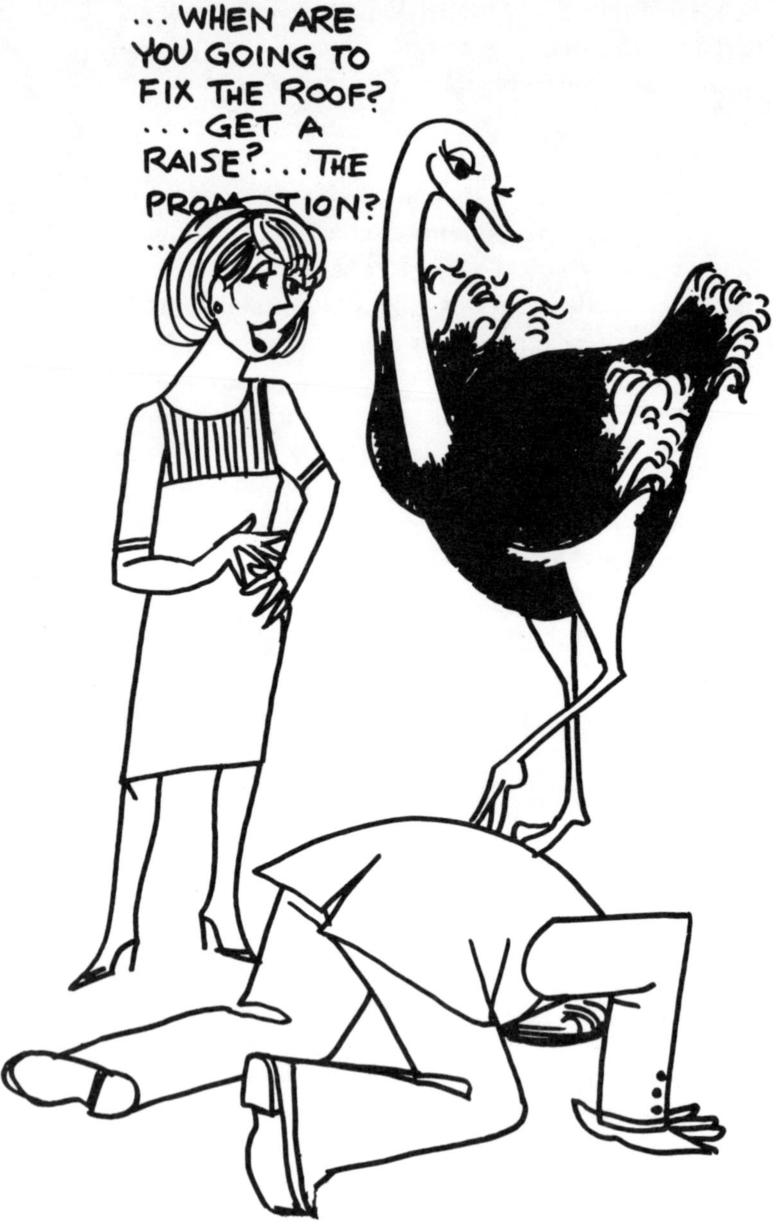
...WHEN ARE YOU GOING TO FIX THE ROOF? ...GET A RAISE?...THE PROMOTION? ...

CHAPTER X

HOW CAN I EFFECTIVELY DEAL WITH CONFLICT?

The world has more than its share of conflicts. The conflicts dealt with in this chapter are on interpersonal conflicts. Assuming that ours is a role oriented society, there will automatically be conflicts when a person begins to be oneself. For clarity's sake, we divide the chapter into two sections: Conflict and oneself and Conflict and others.

CONFLICT AND ONESELF

If you are normal, you will experience conflict when you are on the receiving end of a parent-child communique. Any attempt to decrease your psychological size usually creates conflict. "What do I do? I can't get thru to my husband. He says our marriage hasn't any problems," wails the wife. The message coming through is: My husband puts himself above me; he doesn't seem to think what I say is important.

How do you deal with it? Perhaps, the two most effective tools are *active* listening and being transparent. In this case, you try to understand your husband's feelings. You may feel he is threatened by any communication. If this is the case, you may say something like, "I somehow get the feeling that my wanting to talk to you about what I really feel scares you." It has been my experience that effective or *active* listening has created a common union with the person who seemingly saw himself in a superior role. This approach may work or sometimes it may not.

Being transparent is the other method. The wife might say something like: "I really get up-tight and frustrated when I can't share my feelings with you. I feel ignored and hurt." Notice the use of I instead of the judgmental "you are an insensitive bum." You are being transparent, you are getting your feelings out and hopefully you may get your husband to respond to you as a person. However, you may fail. You then have to decide how hopeful it is to keep on trying. You must choose whether or not you want to continue in a role-to-role relationship, or whether being you and growing as a person is more important than your marriage.

CONFLICT AND OTHERS

Often we find ourselves in a cross-fire or "on the spot" situation between two people. It could be a principal in the middle of a conflict between two teachers, a parent with two of the children, a government counselor caught between an employee and the supervisor.

Dr. Al Main and Dr. Al Roark came up with a consensus model for conflict reduction which certainly may be a useful tool working with conflicts between others. Assuming the ones involved in the disagreement really want to reach a mutually acceptable agreement, you have to point out that you will do what you can on a win-win basis. You will make no judgment on who is right or who is wrong. Your function is to guide the conflictees through the step-by-step process in order to achieve reduction in the conflict.

The conflict reduction model has five steps: (1) the conflictees describe the situation as they see it; (2) the conflictees give a description of how the conflict affects them with regard to feeling and personal meaning; (3) the conflictees give a description of a desired situation to reduce the conflict; (4) the conflictees describe the changes necessary to achieve the situation described in step three; and (5) an agenda or plan of action to reach the desired situation described in step three is outlined.

To illustrate the model in use, a brief example of a conflict resolved through it follows. For brevity the conversation has been edited and condensed. The setting is a disagreement between two ninth grade cheerleaders, Sue and Sally, who were good friends but were on the "outs" with each other. Sue came to me upset about the trouble and I arranged to have the three of us get together to resolve the conflict.

Step One:
Counselor: I want to point out we are not going to establish who's right or wrong but rather try to see what caused the problem and what we can do to solve it. To start with, I want each of you to give me a description of the problem. You don't have to say anything about how you feel; we'll talk about that in a minute. Sally, why don't you start.

Sally: Well, we were friends, I thought, but now Sue won't talk to me and seems to be mad at me and I don't know why.

Counselor: Now, Sue, how about you?

Sue: Yes, I am mad at Sally but it is because of some of the things she has been saying about me and it is causing problems on the cheerleading squad.

Sally: What do you mean by "things" I have been saying about you?

Sue: You've been telling some of the other girls I'm trying to run the cheerleaders and be a "hot dog."

Sally: Yes, I guess I did say some of those things. But I do think you sometimes try to run the cheerleaders.

Sue: I don't mean to try to run the show.

Counselor: Let me summarize what has been said so far. You both agree that Sally has been doing some talking but you disagree that Sue is trying to run the cheerleaders. Does that check with the way you both see it at this point?

Sue: Yes.

Sally: That's right.

Step Two:
Counselor: Now girls, I want you to describe the problems in terms of your feelings.

Sue: I really feel bad about having someone who was a friend talking about me.

Sally: I don't feel good about you being mad at me and I don't feel good about being told what to do all the time in cheerleading.

Sue: I really feel bad about that part. I didn't mean to be so pushy.

Step Three:

Counselor: Now I would like each of you to give a description of how you would like things to be. We'll call this our "desired situation."

Sue: I would just like to be friends again and not have Sally talking about me and not have any problems with cheerleading.

Sally: Yes, I want to be friends again and just not feel like I'm being pushed around in cheerleading.

Step Four:

Counselor: In order to reach our desired situation each of you will have to make some changes. Remember this will have to be a give and take process not a win-lose process. Sue, what do you think you will have to do?

Sue: I guess I have to make sure I'm not trying to be the boss when it comes to cheerleading.

Counselor: O.K. Sally, what changes do you see yourself making?

Sally: I'll have to learn to keep my mouth shut and not talk about Sue to other people.

Step Five:

Counselor: Now let's set up a plan of action to make sure these changes take place. Any suggestions?

Sue: When we started cheerleading we agreed not to have a head cheerleader but maybe we need to elect one so we do have a leader and we know who it is.

Sally: That would be O.K. as long as whomever we elect doesn't get bossy, too.

Counselor: Sally, how would you run it if you were head cheerleader?

Sally: I would have us meet before each game and plan what cheers we are going to do and maybe have each one of us alternate being in charge of the games.

Sue: That sounds good to me.

Counselor: Sally, what about the talking about Sue?

Sally: From now on I will talk to Sue and not about her. I think we should be able to do that.

Sue: I think so, too. That would make me feel better.

Counselor: In order to see if things are going O.K. I want to talk to you girls again. First, you should meet with the other cheerleaders and elect a leader, and then we can meet again. How about Thursday, after the big Wednesday game?

Sally: O.K.

Sue: Sounds good.

Counselor: We'll see then if we need to make any changes in our plan of action.

THE BEST DEFENSE IS A GOOD OFFENSE

What is true in football seems to be true in the area of conflict. You may never be overwhelmed by personal conflict or by conflict of others if you have some tangible plan or offense to deal with it. Hopefully, these two methods will provide you with a good offense.

Dippy?... vhat iss dippy?
Psychology vorks!

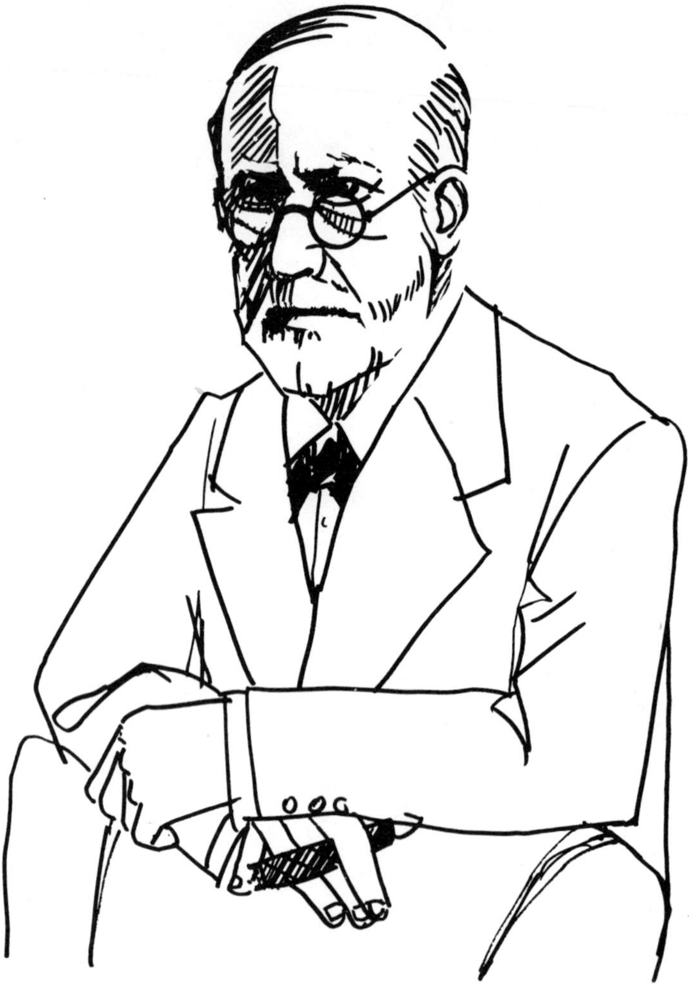

CHAPTER XI

DOES ALL THIS "PSYCHOLOGY STUFF" REALLY WORK IN LIFE?

No doubt you either have heard or have asked this question: does this "psychology stuff" really work? Another popular comment that you may have heard or said: "Half of those psychologists are dippy themselves." Perhaps a clear distinction is necessary. There are a lot of sound and healthy psychological principles but there seems to be some mentally unhealthy people in the field. The opinion that some go into the field of psychology to find an answer for their own problems seems to me to be valid. However, many go into psychology to acquire knowledge and tools to help people in the area of personal growth. The important point is that psychology has a lot to offer people in terms of enriching their lives even though there are some "dippy" people in the field. If one takes a look around, he will find "dippy people" in all walks of life; there are "dippy" principals, "dippy" government workers, "dippy" teachers, "dippy" students, "dippy" mothers and "dippy" fathers. What is essential to remember is that government is good despite some "dippy" government worker, and psychology is good despite some "dippy" psychologists.

1. Does This "Psychology Stuff" Work in Marriage?

One close look at marriage in the United States today indicates that the marriage state has nowhere else to go but up. The soaring divorce rate may also indicate that "doing what comes naturally" isn't working — and perhaps psychology, especially the psychology of communication, may have a lot to say to make the poor marriage good and the good marriage better.

From talking to hundreds of married and divorced people, I've created a theory: "Without the learned skill and attitudes of communication, two people cannot have fulfillment and a truly happy marriage." Perhaps some people are naturally gifted in terms of communication, but most of us have to learn the psychological concepts involved and the skills necessary to make it effective.

MANY MARRIAGES HAVE ROLE-TO-ROLE RELATIONSHIPS

Assuming that we are in a role oriented society, marriages seem to be greatly influenced by roles. There seem to be two major types of roles in most marriages. First, there is the blatant "Dictator-Slave" role. Either the wife or the husband is clearly "the boss." For instance, one person that I know who has a high GS rating in the government has absolutely no say in his home. Secondly, there is the hidden or unconscious "leader-follower" role. The leader gently and tactfully, and often unconsciously, takes all the major decision making. He or she sees this protective role as a responsibility. This seems to be almost a cultural characteristic in the man. He looks at it as merely doing his duty. Often, the woman acquiesces and plays a role of the "good wife." However, the picture below will give you some idea of what takes place.

The psychological gap between the two is tremendous. Playing roles and relating role-to-role is not a growing situation. As was discussed on the chapter on communication, role-to-role relationships are communique and not communication relationships.

The most common answer that I have found for getting divorced was, "I could not be myself in that relationship. I was really playing a role and just could not be myself."

Perhaps the reality of roles in marriage is best brought out by the following letter. This letter is so meaningful that I got permission from the person to use it anonymously.

         July, 1974

Dear Jim,

I have been thinking about what I gained from the class "Enhancing Self-Concept," for five days now. I have been aware of myself and who I am for quite some time now. I am "two people inside constantly battling," but since one of me is slightly weaker it is usually defeated and put back into my subconscious.

The "stronger me" is the normal role-player everyday wife and teacher. It is faithful, kind, humble, naive wife and concerned helpful teacher whose patience and subtle voice relaxes the atmosphere. It comes home from a day of "delightful" children to get supper, clean the house, do the wash, and settle down for 2 hours of television, going to bed right after the news.

The "weaker me" wants to be free, free from roles, expectations, and conformities. It wants to live and get up and go with no concern for any other being. It wants adventure, experience, and probably "immoral" satisfactions. It wants to take off any time with anybody, without checking out with anyone. It wants whatever shall happen or be.

This may be the cause of my sometimes red hot "blow-ups" toward my husband, or my constant dissatisfaction with my work (always wanting to do more and better), or my claustrophobia in the middle of 15-20 children or in a blocked closet giving me the urge to just scream.

So here I am, already tied down to marriage, a new house inhabited for 6 months, and going off the pill in one month. Am I doing the right thing? Or should I get out now before I give birth to any deeper commitments? Would I be happy without my husband, my house, without bearing children? Would I be resentful without complete unrestricted freedom?

I usually tuck the "weaker me" away. This class brought it out again. So here I am. Thanks for listening. A letter makes it easier to talk.

Sincerely,

Anonymous

From the response and "feed back" from this one letter alone, it seems safe to say that "role vs. me" struggle is widespread. After hearing this letter in class one teacher said, "I really thought that I wrote that letter. It was so much in line with what I feel. I have many decisions to make. I love my husband, my kids, my home, job, but I have a new love — ME. I have always been a role but not me. I have been many years in the making. Now what do I do with me? What will my husband do with the new me?"

ROLES AND STRESS

Recently on Barbara Walter's T.V. show there were several experts on stress. They agreed that one of the greatest creators of stress exists when a person has no decision making power. Free will is one of man's greatest dignities. When there is no chance to practice it in real decision making, it is "dehumanizing" and therefore stressful. In a "Master-Slave" or "Leader-Follower" one spouse has a monopoly on decisions. The other is left with "communiques" and stress.

HOW DO YOU GET OUT OF A STRESS ROLE?

First of all, it takes courage and lots of it. It usually takes time to acquire the courage. One housewife in my class shared her experience with the class. For nine years she moved every time her husband decided it was a good "upper" for his job. Presently, she was in a good neighborhood, a good school, and excellent teachers for her children. He decided to move. She, for the first time, stopped playing her role of the "dedicated wife" and said what she felt. She literally grabbed some share of the decision making. She felt that her feelings and her values were important. At that time, the happiness of her children in a "neat" school was more important than 'his making more money. She didn't want to move. What happened? They didn't move. And guess what? Her husband keeps saying, "I really like the new you, Honey." Actually, it wasn't "a new you." Before he only knew a role player, now he knows the real person. This was a switch from "role-to-role" relationships to a growing "I-to-I" relationship. Not all "taking a stand for oneself" will work out as happily. Each one has to weigh the risk involved, for risk is always involved in being yourself.

NON-GROWING CONVERSATIONS

Marriage seems to have the corner on non-growing conversations. Many couples are at the "uh huh" level. This level is exemplified by the husband talking about hunting and the wife responding with "uh huh", and the wife talking about the town gossip and he responding "uh huh." Neither of them either listening or saying anything worth listening to.

One wife got so upset because her husband was giving her the "uh huh" line while he was reading the morning paper at breakfast that she asked, "Dear, would you like the milk on your head instead of your cereal this morning?" He said, "Uh huh," and got a surprise. Another fellow got so tired of his wife ignoring him while she was watching T.V. that he said, "Dear, I fell in love with another woman. Is it okay if I run over and see her?" She said, "Uh huh."

The next level is the role level. "How were things today at work, Dear?" says Lucy. "We got a new fellow and he is really going to work out fine. How was your day at home, Dear?" replies Frank.

The next level is the idea level. Husband and wife discuss ideas about the coming election, or the best way to get family involvement, or how to help in community projects.

The next and highest level is the feeling level. On this level they share themselves through sharing their feelings. This requires a lot of courage. They share their ups and downs, their values, their goals and desires. Unfortunately, most married people never arrive at this level, it seems, and if they get there they don't prolong their stay.

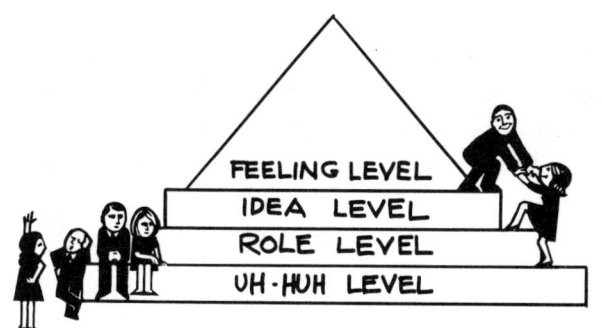

LEVELS OF MARRIAGE CONVERSATION

LEVELS OF MARRIAGE CONVERSATION

PSYCHOLOGY "STUFF" CAN HELP A MARRIAGE

Humanistic psychology says be human by sharing the dignity of decision making with your spouse. Form a sense of belonging and common union through real communication. Aim at moving from the "uh huh" conversation level to the top of the ladder on the feeling level. It also says that you have the RIGHT to be yourself in your marriage. This right includes the right to grow, the right to be loved, the right to privacy, the right to be trusted, the right to be accepted for yourself, the right to be free, and the right to defend yourself. If you will not defend your right to be you, who will? Defending your right to be you takes "loads of courage." Once your defenses of the right to be you are strong, then you can start "having fun being yourself."

II. Does This "Psychology Stuff" Really Work in Raising Children

The thousands of runaways, the thousands of unwed mothers, thousands of juvenile delinquents in America serve notice that the "cupfiller discipline" just doesn't make it.

No doubt, you are aware that "cowboys" don't like hippies. Well, there is a cowboy who was an extremely good "disciplinarian," but his son became a "hippie." Widening the gap of psychological size through moralizing, threatening, ordering, and other "cupfiller" methods usually does more harm than good.

Stanley, a runaway, probably speaks for a lot of runaways when he said, "My parents took away my freedom and power of decision making. I was becoming dehumanized, forced into the mold of my father. I wasn't even allowed to take the classes that I wanted in school. I wanted art, but my parents said that only weaklings and bums were artists. I finally had to 'split' (run away) to preserve my sanity."

THE ANSWER IS IDENTICAL

People who are the most unhappy in a marriage usually seem to have the low role in a marriage. Kids that are unhappy in their families have the low role and sometimes a non-person role in their families. How can this be remedied? Create an atmosphere in which kids feel worthwhile. Disciplining means teaching. Through shared decision making, listening, loving, and communicating with your children you are saying: "Children, you are worthwhile, you have something to offer." Once kids have that worthwhile feeling they will turn out okay. Maybe the real answer is deeper: once parents learn to like themselves and "have fun being themselves" they will create a wholesome growing atmosphere.

The following seven tips based on self-image or humanistic psychology may be keys to create this wholesome atmosphere.

1. Allow kids room to explore who they are and what they can do. Through exploration they are more likely to find something in life that is an extension of their personality.

2. Cultivate independence rather than dependence.

3. Create many chances for decision making.

4. Allow the kids to do everything that they are capable of doing (robbing banks excluded, of course).

5. Let kids grow by allowing them to make mistakes.

6. Let your children get involved with the outside world.

7. Be a "candlelighter" and listen to your children.

About a year ago after the class on active listening, one mother went home and tested it out on her teenager. Next week she came back to class beaming. "For years I have been pounding values into my boy's head. Last night I tried to listen. I never realized what a beautiful teenager I have." And she probably will never realize the impact she made on her relationship with her boy. By seeing him as having a lot to offer, she reduced the psychological size and began to communicate by creating a common union with her boy.

Discipline comes from the Latin and means "teaching," and not "pushing kids around." In regard to child-rearing it means teaching them through your attitudes toward them that they are worthwhile. Through the "Candlelighter" approach, through loving, listening, and communicating with your children, you are clearly saying to them: "Children, you have worth, you have dignity, you have something to offer." Once they see themselves as worthwhile, they will undoubtedly turn out with a lot to give to this world.

The real source of this approach is deeper. Once the parents see themselves as worthwhile, once the parents learn to "have fun being themselves," they will enjoy the experience so much so that they will automatically create an atmosphere encouraging their children to "have fun being themselves."

III. Does All This Stuff Work in Education?

One afternoon several junior high school boys went into a Safeway store in the Denver area. In there they saw their teacher in jeans, buying groceries. They immediately ran outside and shouted to the rest of their buddies, "Hey, Gang, she eats." Years ago (and in some teacher-training colleges today) educators were telling new teachers things like, "Don't smile until Christmas." The assumption being that the more of a hard, strict role you play, the more you have control; the more you have control, the better the teacher you are. Widespread assumptions such as these account for the fact that education is still permeated with role playing. In fact, sometimes it is the chain reaction in role playing. The student plays a role to be accepted by the teacher, the teacher plays a role to be accepted by the principal, the principal plays a role to be accepted by the superintendent. That is the unfortunate chain reaction of role playing. One principal said that he has to wear four hats (four roles); one for the students, one for the teachers, one for the parents, and one for the administration building. Although things are changing in some places, it is definitely still a challenge to be yourself in the educational world.

BUT IT CAN BE DONE

The best psychology teacher I ever had was a young fellow, Dick Usher, at the University of Northern Colorado. Instead of increasing the psychological size between himself and the students, he equalized because he really believed that other people had something to offer. He also took time out the first class to share his background, his identity. He created a "common union" with the students because he could communicate with them in the real sense of the word.

Another person in education was in charge of discipline on the high school level. He was determined to see if he could perform his job without being the "hate" figure. Part of being himself was liking kids and he didn't want to give up that. First of all he used shared decision making in terms of determining the basic rules. Secondly, he respected the students' free will by letting them choose to follow the rules or not. If they did not follow them, they chose the consequences (whatever the group had decided). Thirdly, he was consistent. The result was that he used discipline as a teaching device. The kids felt good because they were in on the decision making. Those who broke the rules realized that they chose the consequences. Consistency safeguarded a "fair shake" for everyone. So instead of the "you got to me, now I'll show you who's boss" discipline which engenders hostility, he created an adult-to-adult discipline which created respect and admiration. It can be done!

One teacher used an inner-action activity aimed at giving the students a good feeling about themselves. She came back to my class and reported that the many pleased looks on her fifth grade children was so exhilarating that this experience was her greatest in teaching.

Halfway, through the class on "Enhancing Self-concept," one teacher became aware that she was actually playing the role of the good teacher who always does what the principal wanted because he must be "older and wiser," otherwise he would not be the principal (another false assumption in education). She became aware that she actually had something to offer in her field of special education. She made an appointment with the principal. Through the attitude of transparency, and the use of "I" statements she shared her ideas, feelings, and suggestions. The principal happened to be very open and desirous of suggestions. In no time, every suggestion was put into practice. The kids were happier! Moreover, the teacher, after nine years of playing a role, took her first big step in being herself which gave her a real "I'm worthwhile" feeling.

One principal has a faculty of eighty teachers in a large high school. A new high school opened in the same district. The administration asked for volunteers to teach in the new school. No one wanted to go. I personally decided to find out why. The most striking reason was that the principal was real and not a role player. His self-image was not dependent on his status as a high school principal. He also really believed that he could learn from others. He sent a note to each staff member to invite their ideas for a better school. He then met with each member individually. At the end, he had a faculty meeting in which they voted on the suggestions of the teachers. His attitude of effective listening equalized the psychological size between the principal and the teachers. The teachers felt a sense of worth and a sense of belonging. Is it any wonder that they were not willing to leave the old high school for the new high school that was headed by an old role player? A real person as principal will do more for the mental health of teachers than a new school with a role player for a principal.

There is no doubt but that it really works in education and it is working. A growing number of teachers are really getting "turned on" to the challenge and rewards of "being themselves." As they "bloom and grow" they will create atmospheres in which children can learn their ABC's, and, at the same time, learn how to "have fun being themselves."

IV. Does This "Psychology Stuff" Work in the World of Work?

Recently a man with a rather challenging position in the government mentioned an experience worth repeating. A supervisor was walking through his office. He said to the supervisor, "How are you? You sure look alive and alert this morning." The supervisor stopped and went over to his desk. He took a piece of paper, wrote the numbers 1, 2, 3. He pointed out that each number has one or more angles. He then paused and said, "What is your angle?" Can you image the atmosphere in the government agency over which this supervisor presides? Distrust, hostility, and revenge must permeate the atmosphere. This government worker has since transferred to another agency. However, he claims that, "Before I retire from the government, I'm going to return the numbers to this supervisor and tell him what he can do with them." This is what happens when the boss increases instead of equalizes psychological size through real communication. Instead of harmony he creates chaos.

Unfortunately, there is no shortage of these "high rolling" role players in positions of authority. There is a fire department captain in particular who treats his men like little children. When every single man under him asked for a transfer, the higher administrator finally transferred the captain. Unfortunately, this captain will create the same atmosphere in the next fire house to which he is transferred.

Attitudes engendered by the "holier than thou" role player are usually those of resentment and retaliation. A classic example is that of one fire chief who constantly "put down" his men so that he could let them know who was the boss in the district. He would even run special classes (inservice) for the different fire stations. He would always ask a hard question which he had looked up the night before. When no one could come up with the right answer, he would let them know how smart he was and how dumb they were by giving the answers.

Examples of people who have power but can't relate to people are all over and in every area of the world of work.

WHY THESE "POOR SUPERVISORS" ARE POOR

From humanistic psychology we can see the probable causes of why some bosses can't communicate. Often in their past experiences they have been "put down" and treated as a non-person themselves. It could have been by their parents or their previous bosses. All they know about management is how they were treated. This vicious circle is exemplified by the boss who said, "This is what I had to do when I was a worker. It was good enough for me, and it is good enough for them. I turned out all right." The assumption that "I turned out all right" could be questioned. In fact there is a well accepted theory that poor bosses don't feel good about themselves. They unconsciously strive for authority to make up for the "not okay" feeling that they have about themselves. They are in the same shoes as the "dippy" psychologist who unconsciously went into psychology to solve his own problems. This psychologist is highly ineffective as a psychologist. Likewise this supervisor is highly ineffective as a boss.

WHAT MAKES A GOOD SUPERVISOR

If a person has the characteristics of a "candlelighter" rather than a "cupfiller" he will, more than likely, be an effective boss. Recently a person who was a real "candlelighter" was transferred to head a department in the state government that was in utter chaos. They had anxiety, hostility, disorder — you name it, they had it. One month after the new boss came the attitude completely changed. One government official said, "You would never know it was the same department." It switched from chaos to harmony. Why? The new boss was a "candlelighter." He established a common union with the people. He listened to them, he understood them, and he gave them a "share in the action" through shared decision making. He didn't hoard "power and authority" to increase psychological size between himself and his staff. Instead he shared the power to create a "team spirit" and common union with the staff.

Recently a young fire captain was promoted to chief. He was a smash success as a captain because he had developed the art of creating a common union with the firemen. As district chief he is the "greatest" (say the men). He is a genius at delegating. He insists on the two major goals: to save lives and put out fires. He delegates to those in charge, i.e., the particular company at the fire. The captains like him, the lieutenants like him, the officers and men like him because he gives them a sense of worth and importance. By "letting them do their jobs" without breathing down their backs, he gives his men the feeling that they are capable and are trusted. By listening to what they have to say, he gives his men the feeling of worth.

YES, THIS "PSYCHOLOGY STUFF" REALLY WORKS!

Our life, school, marriage and work are essentially connected to an inner network of people. Humanistic psychology has a lot to say in terms of using the inner network as fertile ground in which people can grow into beautiful and unique persons that they are capable of being.

Using the tools of a "candlelighter" will help you to grow as a person. What is even better, as you grow to like yourself and "have fun being yourself," you will automatically create an atmosphere in which others can have "fun being themselves."

...cool it, Rev.!

CHAPTER XII

HOW DOES "BEING YOURSELF" JIVE WITH RELIGION

I spent twenty years of my life in the field of religion as a seminarian and a priest. I enjoyed every minute of it. I learned a lot. I also see myself in a good position to make a good marriage between humanistic psychology and religion. I have performed many marriages. None was so much fun and challenging as the marriage between humanistic psychology and religion. I think that the truth is, they are one — so they fit together beautifully.

We have to see clearly that people in the field of religion are human, not divine. Because they are human, they make all kinds of mistakes like you and me. Once we realize this, we can understand the following statement of a young teenage girl. A statement that reflects better than anything I have ever heard, the feelings of literally thousands of teenagers in America today.

CHRIST HAD A LOT OF GOOD IDEAS BUT...

In 1968 a beautiful, intelligent high school girl said to me, "Christ sure had a lot of good ideas, but the Churches sure screwed them up." Her statement seems to reflect a number of young people's attitude toward the Church.

Another young person said, "I know some priests and ministers that are just plain dippy." What is the answer? To me, honesty seems to be the best answer.

There are priests that are dippy, there are ministers that are dippy, and there are rabbis that are dippy. Hopefully, most of them are not. Truthfully, some of them are.

However, dippy people are in every walk of life. There are dippy farmers, but we can't close down the farms. There are dippy psychologists, but we can't throw out psychology. There are dippy principals, but we can't close down the schools. There are dippy policemen, but we can't throw out law enforcement.

As long as we have human beings in the field of religion, we are going to have imperfection. However, we can't throw out the whole concept of religion just because some humans have distorted it.

POPE JOHN SAW THIS

When John became Pope he began to change and renew things. "Let's open up the windows and let some fresh air in," was his reasoning for beginning the Vatican Council. The fresh air brought a lot more freedom and ideas and inter-change into the Catholic Church. He attempted to have the Church grow up from a parent-child relationship where Catholics had to ask permission for everything from the priests, to an adult-to-adult relationship where they would accept responsibility for their own decisions. That is the meaning of the words "Responsible parenthood" movement in the Catholic Church. Actually, John was trying to get Catholics to move away from the role of the child-like, obedient Catholic, to the alive and alert, thinking person using his own God-given mind and will.

RELIGIOUS THINKERS SAW THE NEED FOR IMPROVEMENT

The top notch Christian thinkers realized, like the teenager, that "Christ had a lot of good ideas, but the Churches screwed them up." There have been a lot of wholesome changes in religion in the last twenty-five years.

THE CHANGE IN GOD'S WILL APPROACH

Twenty-five years ago in religious orders, blind obedience was the order of the day. We were taught that you can't go wrong doing God's will. No one would deny that even today. We were also taught that all we had to do was obey our superior and that was God's will. It all sounded nice. However, what if your superior was a neurotic? When I think back to some of the incredible orders of the superiors that were given all under the name of God's will, I remember thinking how God must have felt being blamed for such things. God certainly has a lot of patience. The incidents of Hitler's orders to kill the Jews, and the American's Mai Lai massacre were instrumental in the re-thinking of God's will through blind obedience. Thank God the major thrust in finding God's will is to use our God-given intellect and make most of our decisions by doing the best we can with the talent that God has given us. This is a much more wholesome and mature attitude toward finding God's will than the previous parent-child approach of blind obedience.

THE RE-THINKING OF CHRIST-LIKENESS

Again, twenty-five years ago we were taught that the ideal in life was to be like Christ. No one could disagree with that nobel idea even today. However, as I sit back and recall what that meant in actuality, I see how faulty it was in practice because it really boiled down to nothing more than role playing. I feel that the truth is one. Role playing is bad psychology and poor religion.

How was being like Christ role playing? Very simple. The superior was the one that determined what it was in practice to be like Christ. Consequently, this concept varied with each superior. The truth of the matter was that none of them had a direct line to Christ. As a result, being like Christ meant in practice being just like the superior who interpreted the role of Christ.

Thank God things have changed for the best. At present there is the emphasis toward Christ-likeness and self-actualization as a person. By developing your potential, your talents, your uniqueness as a person, you are imitating Christ who certainly was a self-actualized person. This concept fits so beautifully into humanistic psychology, bringing out the fact that good psychology fits perfectly with good religion.

TO LIVE LIFE MORE ABUNDANTLY

Christ came to earth so that we could live life more abundantly or to the fullest. What better way is there to live life to the fullest than to understand and appreciate your uniqueness as a person. The best way we can show our appreciation of a gift is to use it. I personally can't think of any way to express our appreciation to God for the gift of our person than getting to know and to love ourselves so that we can not just live, but live life to the fullest. In a recent lecture, Dr. Leo Buscaglio summed up this idea beautifully when he said:

"Your life is God's unique gift to you. The way you live your life is your unique gift to God."

RELIGION MEANS HELPING OTHERS TO SEE THEIR WORTH

An essential part of being ourselves as human beings is helping others see themselves in all their glory. Our attitude towards others is directly related to their attitude toward themselves. A friend of mine put it this way:

> We learn to see ourselves
> Through the eyes of others —
> Capable, confident, worthy.
>
> What a great thing we do for others
> When we reflect them to ourselves . . .
> With high esteem, worth, admiration,
> And the realization of their uniqueness.

I had the experience of taking a university class from an agnostic. (An atheist doesn't believe in God; an agnostic believes God is beyond the reach of human knowledge.) This professor, however, valued the uniqueness of each person. He brought out the worth and dignity of everyone in class. He didn't go to Church weekly, but his reverence of the human person was a religious experience. His students learned the subject matter, but beyond that they learned to value themselves as worthwhile human beings. It seems in place to repeat Gregory Baum's famous axiom, "man needs others to become himself." This teacher was the "other" that helped many students become more themselves.

A young elementary teacher in a public school sees children through the eyes of her religious belief system. In her wallet she carries the saying which she tries to live:

> Behold the Christ in every child
> His Divine Perfection
> His ageless soul
> His limitless potential.

This teacher adds a dimension of worth through her view of children. Her children respond enthusiastically. What a difference between her and the teacher who looks upon children as "undisciplined little brats." Helping others to see their worth and love themselves is a beautiful way to bring one's life to religion and bring one's religion to life.

RELIGION MEANS LOVING OTHERS

Loving others is a beautiful way to show our love for God. A "Candlelighter" is geared up to learn to love people. The "Candlelighter" realizes that every person is unique, that every person has something worthwhile to offer. Consequently, he listens to others, to their values, to their thoughts, to their feelings. Through listening, he learns to know them. Through knowing them, he learns to love them. He sees every creature as a small reflection of God's truth, beauty, and goodness. Through open sharing and sincere listening, the "Candlelighter" learns to love many people. He has friends but is open to making more friends because he needs others to be himself. Sharing significant values with others provides him with many peak experiences. He realizes that love is without limit, and he goes through life loving people and making new friends.

Loving others is a religious experience because he sees the goodness of God reflected in humans. He also realizes that it is not a perfect love. He never can be close enough to those he loves. He always has to say goodbye. However, he can accept that because he thinks it is God's way of reminding him that only in Heaven can he find perfection in love. So on one hand, he has the beautiful experience of loving others, while on the other, he accepts its limitations and can say with St. Augustine, "Our hearts were made for you, O Lord, and they will not rest (be fulfilled) until they rest in you."

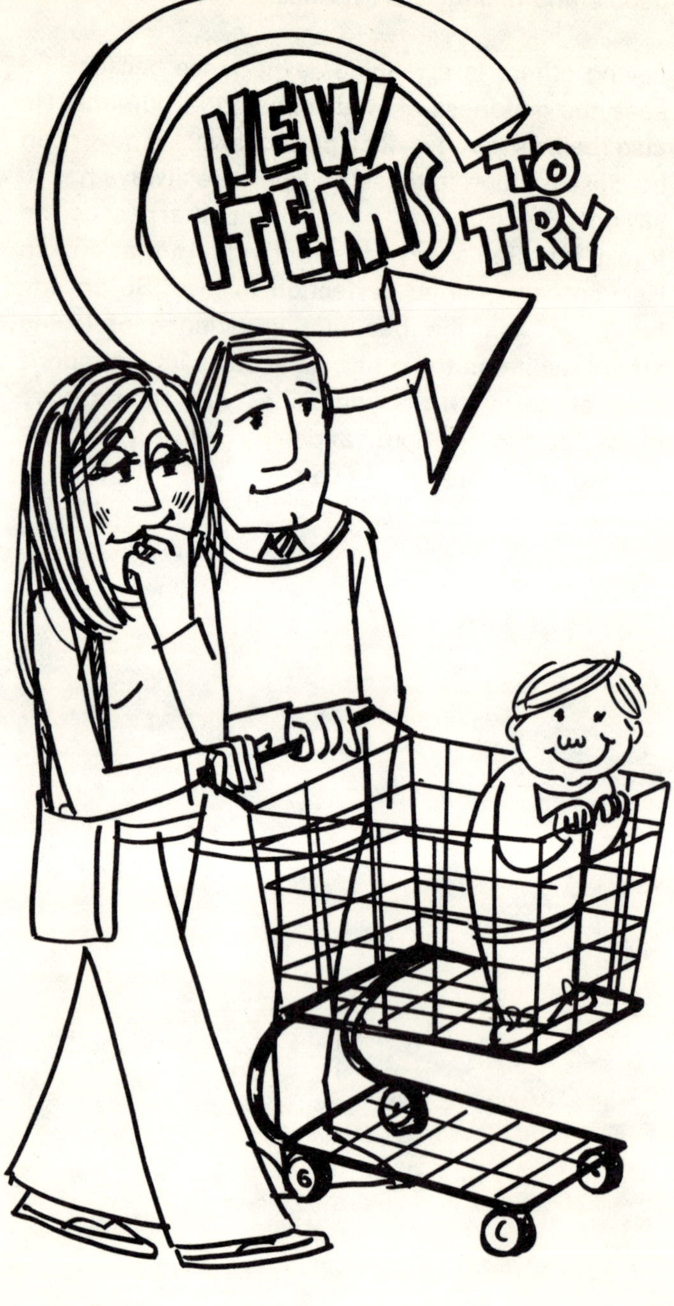
NEW ITEMS TO TRY

CHAPTER XIII

"TRY IT, YOU MAY LIKE IT"

This book, like the "Enhancing Self-concept" class is based on the supermarket approach. It is not the last word or the "cure-all." It has a variety of stock on its shelves from which to choose. You may find something that interests you. Try it, you may like it.

People have taken things from the shelves of this "supermarket of being yourself." The following are just some of the examples of what they did with what they got from the shelves.

Dick, an elementary principal, took the "write me a letter" tool and used it in a different way. He took time to write a letter to each of his staff members in which he commented on some positive contribution that they had made to the school. The response of the teachers was overwhelming. One particular teacher was having a wearing year and was at the point of resigning. The letter renewed her spirit. She changed her mind about resigning.

One mother went home one night and told her teenager about the unusual assignment of writing the teacher a letter. The next morning, to her surprise, there was a letter from her teenager to "Mom." It was the first time Mom knew how her teenager felt because it was too hard for her to speak her feelings, but easy for her to write them. It opened the door to real communication between Mom and daughter. Principals, teachers and counselors all failed to reach a 10-year-old. After all kinds of professional suggestions failed, her father thought he would adapt the "write me a letter" to his daughter. One evening he said, "Honey, I realize that saying what you really feel is hard. How would you like to write what you feel?" The father came back to class the next week overjoyed. It worked. His daughter was able to write her feelings. For the first time this opened the door to communication with his daughter.

A waitress personalized her work through a form of "write me a letter." She, by nature, was extremely friendly. Recently two businessmen went out of her restaurant in high spirits. She'd added a personal touch by writing on the bill, "Real nice having you. Hope you enjoyed the meal. Thanks for stopping here." The men were really impressed. One said, "I've been eating in restaurants all over the country, and this is the first time a waitress wrote a personal note on the check. She really used "write me a letter" in a creative way to humanize and personalize her work.

Another mother went home and adapted the "Happening" to her home. Her teenager was hosting a party for other teenagers. She told her daughter about the "Happening" and she decided that it would be a challenge for her teenage party. It was. She could not get over it. It was the most successful party that they had had at their house. She said, "Usually the kids devastate the house. This time they helped clean up because they were so appreciative."

One teacher took "partners" and tried it every day for five minutes. The effect was amazing. It changed her classroom atmosphere. Kids were forming common bonds, they were listening to each other and the shy ones were beginning to come out of their shells. A man took "partners" and used it at a cocktail party. It turned the party from a typical superficial exchange to a real experience.

Another tried "the big nine marriage line-up" at a party. She said, "I couldn't believe it. Instead of the usual party, it became a meaningful exchange of views on marriage. It was so good — nobody wanted to go home."

Another tried "partners" at her weight watchers meeting. She could not believe how involved people got in the class through "partners." They got to know each other and felt free to participate. She said, "It just isn't the same class." She also said, "I'm using all the ways that will help self-concept because I'm convinced that people overeat because they don't feel good about themselves."

One young man took most of the stuff from the shelves of "having fun being yourself" and incorporated it into his religion program. He shared it with his teachers in a two day workshop. He said that it had absolutely changed the attitudes of the kids. He made religion meaningful. Instead of having to be there, they looked forward to coming.

A young teacher who worked with potential dropouts in a big school district said that he was about to write off the project as a waste of time. He said that the only time that he could get the kids' attention was when he faked an argument with his teaching partner. He shot him with blank bullets. He fell to the floor. The students got up to see what happened. "I can't get over how these "self-concept" things work with these kids," he said. "They really are interested in who they are. I know now that I can finally reach these kids."

A young teacher was upset with the way that the children in her class would "cut" down one another. She tried the "transparency" approach. She said, "Children, I want to share what I feel. I always respect your freedom and your rights. I always wanted to be free to be me and to let others be free to be themselves. I also have rights as a teacher. I personally cringe when I hear 'killer' statements. Therefore, I am going to make the rule of no 'killers' or 'put downs' in this class." She took a stand. She shared a real value. Guess what? She came back to my class literally in "Seventh Heaven." She said that it worked. The whole atmosphere of her class changed. The kids liked it. She shared her honest feelings and got an honest response. No kid likes to be put down. No doubt, they were pleased when the teacher made the "no put-down" rule.

Another man tried the "transparency" approach. He had just finished his degree and was substitute teaching until his full time contract began in six months. He was subsituting in a junior high school where the kids were famous for "wiping the floor" with substitute teachers. He was aware of this. He walked into the class. He took five minutes to share his feelings, to be transparent. He said, "I really get the feeling that you would like to give me a work out today. When I was your age I felt and did the same things. However, I am really caught in a bind. I've got a wife and two little boys, 3 and 4 years old, to support. I really have no steady job. Until September I will have to depend on substitute teaching. This means that I have to do a good job so that I will be called back. I would like to present an offer to you. Let's see if we can get through the work the teacher left us to do. In the last ten minutes, then, we can do some fun communication games which you'll really like." His substituting on the junior high level went as smooth as clockwork. He was transparent, he was real — kids responded beautifully. It worked for him.

A teacher of an adult education class was warned by the coordinator that there was one person who had torn into every teacher for the last two years. It was simply a case of psychological size. The student had to look bigger and smarter than the teacher. The teacher decided to see if the tool of active listening could equalize the psychological size. He took an opportunity to talk to the man after class, and actively listened for 45 minutes. The teacher enjoyed it because the man had a lot going for him. What is more significant is the fact that the listening established a common union. It equalized the psychological size. At the end of the class the one-time trouble maker told the teacher that this was one of the best classes that he had ever attended.

One young principal used the tool of active listening for both teachers and parents. He was amazed at the results. Many times he had no solution for the problems. His ability to really understand and listen gave them the courage to accept things that they could not change. He said, "Listening is the greatest tool that I have as a principal."

A mother thought that she would try "shared decision making and listening" with her five-year-old child. He had received some money for his birthday.

She took him to the store, gave him his $5.00 and let him choose the shoes that he wanted. His choice was totally different from what she would have chosen. She made a different suggestion, but he knew and chose what he wanted. The beam of worth, happiness, and dignity was reflected in her little boy's face. The mother said, "I never thought of listening to my children and letting them decide little things like picking shoes. I'll be listening and looking for opportunities where my children can make choices instead of my deciding for them."

A middle-aged man thought he would try active listening with his wife. He came home from work, asked his wife how she was. She said fine. He was listening for feelings and he found that from her voice and appearance she looked upset instead of "fine." He said, "I know that you said 'fine,' Dear, but you look upset." He hit the feeling perfectly. She replied, "You're right. I had a bad day. The kids were unbearable. Your turning on the radio at breakfast woke them too early and they really are crabby when they don't get their sleep." He came back to class thrilled. He was glad that he learned how to get at his wife's feelings. They talked about the radio and the kids. The next morning he kept the radio volume down. "Before this," he said, "she would always repress her feelings under 'I'm fine.' I would always feel uncomfortable so I would end up drinking with the boys. This listening tool may be the key to communication in our marriage."

There was another mother who used active listening to change her appraoch to her pre-school age boy. She used to say, "Billy, just do it this way — it's easy."

Then, she began to think about looking at if from Billy's world. Telling him that it is easy has a discouraging effect. If he makes it, he has no sense of accomplishment. If he fails, it is a disaster because it was easy and he could not do it. This young mother learned to see life from Billy's world.

A young man thought that he would take the "transparency" tool off the shelf and give it a try with his next door neighbor whose dogs were always frightening his little children. He said, "Joe, I really have a problem with my little children. I can't get them outside in the yard to play because they are frightened by your dogs." Joe, completely unaware of this, replied, "You know, Dave, I never realized that. Maybe we could go in together and put up a fence." The problem was solved in harmony and he and the neighbor have become much more friendly. Dave said, "Thank God, I ran across the transparency approach, because I was just about ready to use my judgmental approach. I was going to tell him, 'Keep those damn dogs locked up or I'll call the dog catchers!' If I'd done that, I'd have no fence and bitter feelings instead of harmony."

One realistic person tried out a lot of the ways of "having fun being yourself" and it changed his life's plan. He had done extremely well in real estate. He had planned the next year to retire at 44 and travel around the world. He could live on his investments. From trying out these things designed to help him find out who he was and where he was going, he said, "Dammit, this ruined my travel plans. I found out that part of me was helping people. Helping people brings me happiness. Going around the world was basically helping myself. I have changed my plans."

Another young housewife used the "transparency" approach in a very real way. Every time she received a phone call while she had company she suffered. She felt that she should be with her company, but she didn't want to offend her caller. For years she suffered this wearing anxiety, hoping that her caller would say goodbye. She tried being real (or being transparent) and IT WORKED. Now when she receives a call in this situation, she immediately says, "Gee, I'm really glad you called. I've got a lot to talk about, but I have company right now. How about calling you back in about an hour?" She did the balancing act and it worked. She was real. She felt that she should stay with her company, and she did. She did not want to lose her sense of belonging (friendship) with her caller, and she didn't. She was herself, she was transparent, and it did a lot to reduce unnecessary anxiety in her life.

One young teacher had a fifth grade class which, she felt, had poor self images. She "accentuated the positive letter." She had the students work in groups of six. Each one received five letters (a sentence or two) on one positive aspect seen by the others. Each one was given equal time to compare it with how he saw himself. Most of these kids didn't know that they had anything going for them. She said, "The glow from these kids lit up the room." For her it was the peak expereince of her teaching career.

One counselor took all the items off the shelves of the Supermarket of Self-Concept and brought these items to her faculty. First she did them in the classroom for the teachers. They were so enthusiastic that they spent one hour a week after school with the counselor in sharing the "ways of having fun being yourself" with the staff.

One woman took a lot of things from the shelf and tried them with herself and her family. She viewed it all in terms of one of her major goals for the last twenty years. She joyously and confidently said, "I now can lose weight because I see myself as worthwhile. I've tried to lose weight for twenty years unsuccessfully because I saw myself as a 'not okay' person. I was never aware of the cause of my lack of success."

Another young mother changed her style of life to a certain extent by doing the "Time Pie." She realized that she had hardly any time for herself. She said, "Since the time pie, I cut a piece out for me and it really has added a dimension to my life. Funny how one simple exercise opened my eyes and changed my life!"

One teacher was in charge of a teachers' meeting and she used the creative name tags. She felt it was a tremendous meeting because the making and sharing of name tags for twenty minutes really relaxed the atmosphere, broke up the cliques, and got people to know each other.

One husband realized that his marriage conversations were more role-talk or busy-talk than deep level sharing. He and his wife have made a change. Instead of reading the morning paper, they each have equal time to share their last twenty-four hours' of feelings — their uppers and their downers. They both enjoy it so much that they miss it when the husband has to be out of town. It took courage at first, now it is on the level of "having fun being yourself."

He said, "We used to share things through sharing ideas. Now we share ourselves through sharing feelings. Our marriage was static, now it is a growing one."

One wife took the "seeing self collage" home and did it with her husband. She came back to report that they both learned more about each other doing that than they had in their first five years of marriage.

Some have taken everything off the shelves of "Ways of having fun being yourselves." Over the period of ten weeks they have been themselves in a different light. Their results were reflected in the statement of one who wrote, "I realized I have really been playing a role. In fact, the work I was doing was really fulfilling others' expectations. I know much more about me and where I want to go. I am now in the process of changing my career to one which fits me as a person."

One of the most striking examples of "having the courage to be oneself!" is that of a fellow named Stan who was an ex-boxer. It was the last class. Those who so wished were explaining their "seeing self collages." The class was about over when he said, "I didn't do a collage. Instead I wrote a poem. I would like to read it."

Branches are many
Limbs are few
A trunk is strong and contains the
Heart of life
But there is only one.

*Leaves are my display
But they are temporary.*

*The wind may tear my branches
Until there are few.*

*The leaves come and go as they please
Turmoil may strip my limbs
Until there are none
But only myself or God may
Destroy my trunk.*

*Therefore I may always
Start again if I wish.*

While reading the poem he was shaking like a leaf. After he read it, everyone wanted a copy. I talked to him later. He said, "Jim, that was the hardest thing that I did in my life. It took more courage to read my poem than all the boxing matches in my life. I was sharing myself and if anyone had laughed, I never would have been able to return to a class like this." No one laughed. It was the first time Stan had shared a poem with anyone. Everyone was richer that day because he had the courage to share his uniqueness, his self.

REACHING OUT BEYOND THE CLASSROOM

Many people gave these "ways of having fun being yourself" a try — and they liked them. There are those who have experienced them in the classroom and in workshops. Over the past three years these amount to only 1600 people. The book has as its purpose to break out of the walls of the classroom to reach to people who will never go to a classroom. This book will give a lot of everyday people a chance to brouse through the "Supermarket of Self-Concept" and pick out some relevant things from the shelves filled with "ways to have fun being yourself."

APPENDIX

WAYS TO "HAVE FUN BEING YOURSELF"

The following are ways that have been tried in education, in government, and in the world of work. They can be adapted to fit any age group. Teachers have used them in the classrooms, parents have used them in the home, and consultants have used them in workshops for government and business. They work in all walks of life helping people "have fun being themselves."

1. The Time Pie
Draw a pie. Divide it into two parts. One part represents the amount of time you spend doing what others want you to do. The other part represents the amount of time you spend doing what you like to do. Then, draw another pie on how you would like it to be.

Example From an Actual "Pie" of a Class Member

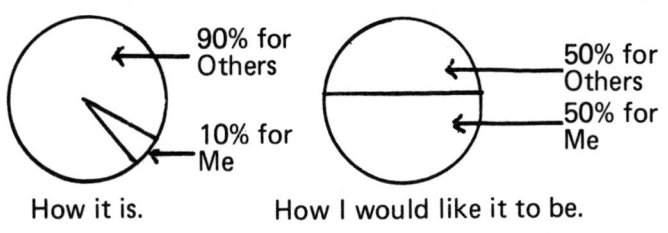

90% for Others
10% for Me
How it is.

50% for Others
50% for Me
How I would like it to be.

2. Partners
This fulfills the basic need to belong as well as learning about who we are. Designed originally to be used in the classroom in order to help students learn to express themselves, to listen, to think about themselves on a deep level, and to develop a sense of belonging. It has been used at parties, workshops and

conferences. Each person has a partner. A topic is given. The partners have four minutes to discuss the topic. Each one has a chance to speak and to listen. After four minutes, they change partners. They change every four minutes until each one has a chance to talk with every person in the class or group or until time runs out. Create the topics beginning with easy ones to more challenging ones. The following are examples of topics that have been successful:

1. A favorite thing growing up.
2. Your hobby.
3. Your goal for this year.
4. The best things you like about your job.
5. The best thing you like about your family.
6. The best thing you like about yourself.
7. What do you do when you are depressed.
8. Something you want to accomplish before you die.
9. The best thing you like about your best friend.
10. The best thing you like about your boss.

If there is a large group, just create more thought provoking topics. If it is a special group, create topics tailored to the group, e.g., for married couples.

1. The time you decided to get engaged.
2. Your goal as a couple.
3. The thing you think most essential about your marriage.
4. The quality you like best about your spouse.
5. The quality you think your spouse likes best about you.
6. What you would like to change in your spouse.
7. What you think your spouse would like to change in you.

Partners, this one to one conversation on meaningful topics, is one of the most effective ways to start people off on the road to who they are and where they want to go.

3. Who Am I?
Answer this question on a paper. Below is a common answer.

1. I am a man.
2. I am a husband.
3. I am a government worker.
4. I am a father, etc.

Since this tells nothing about you to others or to yourself, repeat the exercise using only traits or personality characteristics like the following example:

1. I am somewhat shy.
2. I am fun loving.
3. I am a sharing person.
4. I am curious.
5. I am daring.
6. I am sometimes a bright red balloon.
7. I am sometimes a black cloud.
8. I am sometimes a misty morning.
9. I am sometimes a sunset behind Long's Peak.

4. Win, Place or Show
Knowing what you like is another clear way to know something more about yourself as a person. Win, place or show will help you learn to see more clearly things that are important in your life.

Write 18 things that you like to do as fast as you can. Catagorize them according to the following letters or symbols:

W   beside the one you like the best
P   beside the one you like the second best
S   beside the one that comes in third
$ beside the ones which cost over a dollar each time you do them, e.g., movies
D   beside the ones you do when you are depressed
R   beside the ones you still can do when you retire
A   beside the ones you do usually alone
O   beside the ones you usually do with others
E   beside the ones you usually do enough
NE beside the ones you usually don't do enough

(You can create more categories easily.)

Once you have finished the catagories, you may do it again in terms of how you would like it to be. For instance, if you find that there are some things you like but do not do enough, you may want to set some goals to change that. This is a very practical way to make progress on the road to "having fun being yourself."

5. Take a Stand

This is a neat way to help people become aware of how they feel, take a stand on how they feel, and accept others who feel differently. This fits well into the classroom or a party setting.

Make five signs and pin them on the wall.

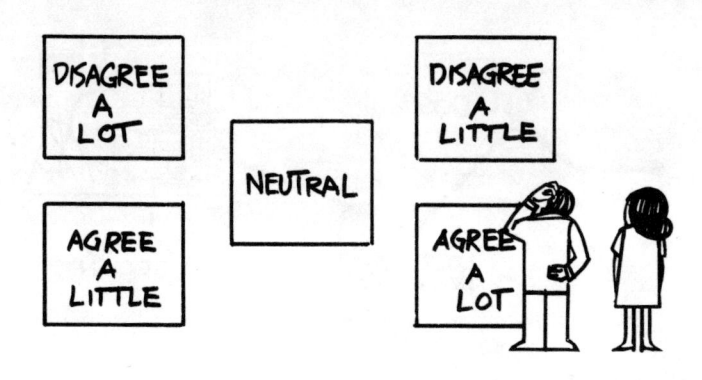

Next make up some relevant statements and have people stand in line with the sign that expresses their feelings. Some sample statements are:

1. Streaking is a wholesome activity.
2. Trial marriages are good.
3. Capital punishment should be restored.
4. There should be one boss in each family.
5. Women are discriminated against in the business world.
6. Most people do not really know their spouse before marriage.

Have the people in the group or in the class make up similar statements. This is a fun way of allowing people to be themselves by standing up for what they feel.

6. Emotional Heart Beat
This way consists in tracing your feelings from birth until the present with emphasis on the major uppers and downers. For example:

The sample graph has getting a dog as an upper. The dog got lost and that is a downer. He began school and that was an upper. He merely would continue the graph, e.g., marriage, divorce, etc., right up until the present date. The assumption of the Emotional Heart Beat is simple: we can learn from the past. An increased awareness of where we have been may help us understand where we are as well as where we want to go.

7. Name Game
Making a game of learning names is fun and builds a good atmosphere in the class or at a party. Actually there are two name games. The first one is based on a psychology that emphasizes the importance of drill or repetition. Start with the first four names. Ask for a volunteer to repeat those names. Then the first four repeat their names adding another person. Another volunteer repeats the five names. Continue until everyone is included. When several have been able to name everyone, change places and see if they can do it.

The second name game is based on perceptual psychology. Each one tells how he feels about his name. Jim may say, "I never liked my formal name, James, because it was always the name of the butler in movies when I was growing up. I prefer just plain Jim."

It is amazing how these two games relax the atmosphere, help people feel at ease, and help them learn about each other.

8. Creative Name Tag
At a party, conference, class or church social have different color paper, scissors, and pins. Let people design their own name tags. You'll be surprised at the variety because it is a practical outlet for them to "have fun being themselves."

Another way is to have them print three material things they value on their name tag. It is a simple and fun way in which people can form bonds, break the ice, and have more fun at a gathering while learning more about who they are.

9. Supermarket of Self-Concept
Create some categories taken from life, e.g. plane, train, ship, sailboat, bike, roller skates, car. In a classroom situation, place signs of each mode of transportation around the room. First, ask the children to think how they see themselves. Then ask them to go to the thing that best expresses them. When they get there, they can choose a chairman. He, in turn, reports back to the group why their group saw themselves as "Sailboats." This really enables kids to think about who they are. Next you can tell them to go to the one they think others would put them. After that they can go to the one that they would like to be. Aside from having fun, they learn a lot about the different self-concepts, e.g., how they see themselves, how they think others see them, how others see them, and how they would like to be. One boy said, "I see myself as a train because I am slow and steady and reliable.

However, I'd like to be a plane because I'd like to be more free, to go in different directions, to go fast, to glide." This boy is beginning to come alive by being somewhat aware of who he is and who he would like to be.

10. The Big 10 in Marriage
This is an excellent way to get people to line up what really is important in a marriage. Just give them the following things and have them put them in order of importance to them from one to ten: money, status, children, sex, job, friends, communication, companionship, security, religion. Have each line them up separately. Afterward, they can compare to see how many they put in the same order. This would be ideal for people thinking of marriage, to check out where they stand on important values in marriage. All things being equal, studies indicate that the more alike in values, the happier the marriage will be. With a little creativity one could make a "Big 10" for students, for singles, etc.

11. The Communicating Picture
This way is amazing as well as fun. Get into groups of from two to four. One box of crayons per group. The group draws a picture together *without talking*. They are given 15 minutes to complete it. Afterwards each group has a chance to share their feelings about their art work. It is amazing to see the degree of communication that takes place without words.

12. The Puzzle Art Work
Cut the paper into four pieces. Give each member a piece. Each one draw a picture of what this world really needs. After each picture is complete, each individual returns to the group and helps put the pieces together. They then talk about the results. Art is really

a means for people to express themselves and learn about themselves.

13. Home-Work Buildings
Draw an outline of a home. Divide it in half, In each half symbolize an important value in your home life. Do the same thing in work. Below is an example:

A. HOME

The values symbolized here are this man's two little boys. The value on the right symbolizes his communication with his wife.

B. WORK

The symbol at the bottom of his office is a tree representing how he does things that spread out and influence many others. On the top is a smiling face representing his boss who trusts him and smiles pleasingly at the work he is doing.

Give the people time to discuss their art work. This way provides them with increased awareness of what is important to them in life. This can be adapted to any group, e.g., if used in school, have the students do the values at home and at school.

14. One Chance Question
This way really helps people think as well as reach a level of conversation that is "growing talk" instead of "small talk." Divide up in threes or fours. Each person gets a chance to be interviewed. The others have only one question each. The goal is to try to ask a question by which the questioner can learn some important value. The person being interviewed can pass over any question he doesn't wish to answer. One could ask the question, "Where were you born?" or "What is your goal for the next year?" The first question is "small talk." The other is "growing talk." The response to this One Chance Question has been nothing short of tremendous. It really is a powerful tool for people to explore things that are important in their lives.

15. Accentuate the Positive Plan
The purpose of this way is to enable people to see how others see them, and to compare it to how they see themselves. It is safe because it is limited only to the positive. It helps people learn how others see them. It makes them aware of what they have going for them. It also helps them see two self-concepts in action: how they see themselves and how others see them.

Divide up into groups of five. Each one writes down on a piece of paper one positive thing he sees in each of the other people, e.g., "John, you seem to be very friendly." Each one receives all his mail. He, then, compares it with how he sees himself. Each has a couple of minutes to share his reactions about his mail. This has been a very effective tool in growing in self-knowledge.

16. Creative Animals
This seems to be a favorite with younger students, but it is fun and a learning experience for all ages. Give each a sheet of paper. Divide up in groups of four or five. Each one attempts to tear out an animal from the sheet of paper. The person chooses the animal that best represents himself. Each has a chance to explain his choice. One boy said, "I'm a puppy because I am friendly and I like to be hugged." This is a fun way to get kids to start thinking about who they are.

17. Candle Lighting
Actually this way consists of practice in listening effectively, the essential quality of a candlelighter. This is done in two's. Ditto a sheet of paper with feeling-provoking, incomplete sentences. One party completes the sentence. The other tries to understand perfectly both the words and the feelings, i.e., he tries to listen on both channels. When the speaker is satisfied that he is fully understood on both channels, he takes his turn listening to the other until he feels that he is completely understood. Ten or twelve good incomplete sentences will keep the activities going for hours. Below are some examples of feeling-provoking sentences:

1. When my favorite team loses a game, I feel —
2. When I am in a new group, I —
3. At a cocktail party, I usually —
4. When I am being blamed for something, I —
5. When I get depressed, I usually —
6. When I have time alone, I —
7. When someone forgets my name, I feel —

8. When I think of the millions who will starve in the world this year, I feel —
9. When someone compliments me, I feel —
10. When someone ignores me, I feel —

Practicing candle lighting or effective listening is essential. This way is so involving that people have gone right through coffee breaks. Incomplete feeling-provoking sentences can be created to fit any class or group.

18. The Best First Line Up
This is a good way to start thinking about what is important to you. Just compose three items, ask the class or group to line them up with the best first. For little kids things such as: ice cream, bike riding, T.V. cartoons, swimming, etc. For teenagers the list could include: dancing, hot rods, talking on the phone, movies, etc. For adults the list could include: going out for dinner, cocktail parties, golf, bridge club, etc. The idea is to help people clarify what is important to them.

19. The Worst First Line Up
This way just approaches clarifying what is important from a different view. A couple of examples will do, e.g., for a teenager getting into a wreck with his Dad's car, getting arrested for stealing, and getting kicked out of school. Line up the worst first if you were married and the following could happen: your spouse gets fired from his/her job, your house burns down and the insurance had expired by accident, your spouse goes to the class reunion, drinks too much and gets "smashed" and has a "one night stand" with his/her old high school flame. This creates fun and learning at the same time and can be used at a party, in the classroom or with most groups.

20. Self-Concept Collage

This is a beautiful option to writing a term paper for a college psychology class. It can be adapted to any level of education. Basically, it consists of finding pictures and things from magazines that resemble you, and arrange them into a collage. One of the most common comments is: "I've never put so much time into a project, had so much fun, and learned so much about myself." In class the collage is due the final evening of class. Sharing collages has given many people a real peak experience in terms of knowing themselves and getting to know others.

21. Where I Am and Where I Want To Be

This way can be adapted to many areas. It consists of a line with two marks. One mark indicates "Where I am," the other indicates "Where I want to be." This could be used in various areas: personal, career and family.

Example:

This is taken from a real person who was a fireman 13 years ago, and today is a district chief. It gives one a clear picture of his or her goal. The trick about making this work is to find the obstacles to your goal. Then make the removing of the obstacles your immediate goal. It is based on the assumption that life is precious. Therefore, it is worth taking time to find out just how we want to spend our lives.

THE "WHY" OF WAYS

These ways are fun, but too powerful to be called games. They have changed people's lives just by getting them started in thinking about who they are and where they want to go. They are fun, but they are powerful. I just can't help but think of the glowing faces of school kids taking part in "partners." It seems that a lot of them were being listened to for the first time in their lives. Then there was the young, formerly married woman who started to change her whole style of life once she did the time pie and realized that she was short-changing herself.

The twenty-one "Ways" are basic tools. You can adapt them, change them, use them as stepping stones to new ways. These "Ways" are in this book because so many teachers have said, "Yes, I am in favor of kids having good self-concepts, psychologists are in favor of it, parents are in favor of it, but how do I go about it?" Hopefully, these twenty-one ways fulfill these needs for teachers. However, these ways have gone beyond the classroom to workshops in education, government, and business, to families, and to social events and parties. If they work for you, share them with someone. Light someone's candle so that they can learn to not "just live," but to come "alive" through these ways of "having fun being yourself."

GETTING IN THE LAST WORD

Dear Reader,

It is February 11, 1975, 10:00 p.m. I just finished the last chapter. Never in my life have I been tied down as I have been the last three months trying to get this book finished.

What a neat, oneness, wholesome feeling it is to know that I did something I had to do! One part of me is sharing helpful things with others. I've come across some wonderful things in my life that have helped myself and people in my classes live a fuller life. Now, these ways of "being you" have made it beyond the walls of the classroom.

There is another part of me. I like to be free! I published this book through Communications Unlimited because I didn't feel like giving up my freedom to the many rules and regulations of a publisher. I just wanted to share what I had to share in my loosely organized way.

I really feel that I am more *me* after this book. I said everything I feel strongly about! This has given me a whole feeling and a real experience of having fun being me.

I had to share these neat feelings I have in completing this book. I hope that you got as much from reading it, as I did from writing it.

Sincerely,

P.S. Number 1: I just picked up my copy from the 16-year-old boy who did the proof reading for me. After reading the book, Brad Pierson wrote this poem for me, and I want to share it with you.

To start, you need to finish.
   A beginning needs an end.
Wheels continue but never start.
   So what about life?

Life has a start and a beginning.
   It has an end and finish.
It shall always continue, but
   Where does it start?

Does it start at birth
   Or at death?
Or does it start when you realize
   There is something for you to accomplish?

When you think about it,
   Are you alive?

P.S. Number 2: Just wound up a class on "Enhancing Self-Concept." Guess what? I have another neat poem which I just have to share. The creativity of people is so beautiful! Listen to this:

A RECIPE OF ME

a lot of heart
a reasonable amount of brains
a quantity of tongue
a goodly portion of ham
a sizeable measure of corn

part crab
part honey
sweet and sour
a low boiling point
sometimes in a stew
flaky
very mushy at times
sometimes fresh, but not raw
never pickled
no good when whipped
needs to be buttered up occasionally
must be "kneaded" or will fall
better warm than cold
improves with age
serves many

                              Dorothy Stone

P.S. Number 3: If after reading this book, you are interested in more information or in workshops in your area (education, government, or business), please write or call me at:

    Communication Unlimited
    7057 Wright Court
    Arvada, Colorado 80004
    Phone: 303-424-4957

We endorse the concept of competency based education. All of our workshops are competency based. If the majority of participants do not feel that the workshop is worthwhile, there is no charge.

THANKS TO EVERYDAY PEOPLE

Through this book people have shared their lives and their stories with others. "People helping people are the luckiest people in the world" is the story of the success of this book.

I would love to recall the names of all those who made this birthday edition possible. Thanks to Gary Giann who engineered its printing and whose creativity comes out so well in the finished product. Thanks to Dee who helped with the proof reading along with my Mom. Thanks to the many letters of appreciation for writing the book. Thanks for the letters of those who explained how the book has made their lives more meaningful. Thanks to those who personally promoted the book by sharing their copy with friends or giving the book for birthday and Christmas presents. Thanks to the many who send in orders for this book from all over the U.S. and abroad. Thanks to Joe whose gentle push in 1974 provided the impetus for the first edition of this book. Thanks to Kathy who in 1973 asked me for a copy of my notes on "self image." I had scatter notes. Her question gave me the motivation to put my notes together in the form of this book.

As I sit here typing I cannot but think how nice it would be to have a photographic memory by which I could recall everyone who helped make this book a reality. I also want to thank the future readers of this book who find it so helpful that they share it with their friends instead of putting it in their library.

Finally, since this is a book for everyday people, my sincere appreciation to the everyday people, all over the country, who allowed their struggle to be themselves to become the core of this book.

Many people in the underdeveloped nations are starving physically. The gigantic task to feed them leaves the everyday person feeling helpless. In the developed country of America, millions of people are half-starved psychologically. They have satisfied their need to belong by playing roles, but they starve their need to be themselves by repressing their real feelings. Their values seem to be topsy-turvey: "HAVING IS NO. 1, DOING IS NO. 2, AND BEING COMES IN LAST." Having equal roles, e.g., having a wife, having a husband, having children, having status, or having a big house. Doing is how you acquire the "having." Work, achieve, move up the ladder so you can rank high in the "having" department. Being is a necessity only in terms of the fact that you have to be alive in order "to do" so you are able "to have."

Philosophically, things are upside down. Being, according to the world's great thinkers, is being No. 1. Since each person is unique, his being is by far the greatest thing a person has to offer.

Hopefully, this book will help many people eliminate psychological starvation through suggesting ways of "Having Fun Being Yourself."

To all those who made the book possible, I sincerely want to say THANKS.

May God bless you always and in all ways.

Communication Unlimited is a vibrant and growing company. Aside from publishing books, the staff conducts workshops on stress reduction, management effectiveness, communication and related areas. If after reading this book you are interested in more information, write or call:

>Communication Unlimited
>7057 Wright Court
>Arvada, Colorado 80004
>(303) 424-4957

A sampling of clients of Communication Unlimited:

Johns-Manville World Headquarters - Denver
FAA - Salt Lake
Gates Rubber Company - Denver
Civil Service Training - Panama
Hawaiian Educational Council - Honolulu
VA Hospital - Fargo
Bureau of Reclamation - Salt Lake
Board of Realtors - Lakewood
Chamber of Commerce - Wheatridge
University of Hawaii - Honolulu - Maui - Kauai
Metropolitan State College - Denver
University of La Verne - La Verne
US Customs - Regional Office - New Orleans
Rockwell International - Boulder
Department of Energy - Albuquerque
Altus Air Force Base - Altus
Camp Carson Army Base - Colorado Springs
Colorado Association of School Administrators - Denver
American Operating Room Nurses Convention - St. Louis
Federally Employed Women Convention - Denver
Samsonite Corporation - Denver
Public Service Company of Colorado

THREE BOOKS TO COPE WITH STRESS

Jim Keelan writes for "YOU, INC."
"Nobody says it better."

1. **THE WORLD OF STRESS**

B-1 **B.S.* & Live Longer:** *(Beat Stress) August, 1978. This is a creative approach to coping with stress. Backed with strong research, the book quotes hard statistics which are complemented by first hand testimonials around stress experiences. The major focus is on stopping up the **Stress Generators** as well as identifying tools and techniques for **Stress Reduction.** $4.95

2. **A MAJOR STRESS GENERATOR FOR MANY.**

B-2 **Re-Entry into the Single Life:** 1977. The book addresses the chaos of guilt and fears experienced by the divorced and the widowed. The author guides the reader through three steps, aiming toward achieving the status of being a complete person and removing the barriers to future relationships. $4.95

3. **A MAJOR STRESS GENERATOR FOR EVERYONE.**

B-3 **Having Fun Being Yourself:** 1975. This book was written to help YOU get to know and to like YOU. There is an orderly progression toward recognizing your values and identifying as either a "cupfiller" or a "candlelighter." The author addresses truth... the kinds of truth that will make you free to have fun being yourself. $4.95

To Order Books by Dr. Keelan, write to:
  COMMUNICATION UNLIMITED
  7057 Wright Ct.
  Arvada, CO 80004
  (303) 424-4957

Cost: Each book is $4.95, plus .75 for postage and handling.

Information on workshops on stress management, communication strategies, and cassette tapes offered by Communication Unlimited may be obtained by contacting Dr. Keelan at the above address.

BOOKS YOU MAY FIND HELPFUL

As Man Thinketh, by James Allen
Born to Win, by Muriel James and Dorothy Jongeward
I Ain't Much, Baby, But That's All I Got, by Jesse Lair
The Little Prince, by Antonie de Saint Exupery
Love and Laughter, by Marjorie Holmes
Notes to Myself, by Hugh Prather
On Becoming a Person, by Carl Rogers
Parent Effectiveness Training, by Thomas Gordan
The Prophet, by Kahlil Gibran
Jonathan Livingston Seagull, by Richard Bach
The Transparent Self, by Sidney Jourard
T.A. for Tots, by Alvyn Freed
Values Clarification, by Sidney Simon, Leland W. Howe and Howard Kirschenbaum

Books by Dr. Jim Keelan
* Having Fun Being Yourself
* Re-entry into the Single Life
* B.S. (Beat stress) and Live Longer

To order books by Dr. Keelan, see page 183.

COMMUNICATION UNLIMITED
7057 Wright Court
Arvada, Colorado 80004
(303) 424-4957